# Johann Sebastian Bach

## and the Art of Baroque Music

# Johann Sebastian Bach

## and the Art of Baroque Music

Donna Getzinger

Daniel Felsenfeld

**MORGAN
REYNOLDS**
*Publishing, Inc.*

620 South Elm Street, Suite 223
Greensboro, North Carolina 27406
http://www.morganreynolds.com

# Classical Composers

Johann Sebastian Bach

Antonio Vivaldi

Richard Wagner

Johannes Brahms

George Frideric Handel

JOHANN SEBASTIAN BACH AND THE ART OF BAROQUE MUSIC

Copyright © 2004 by Donna Getzinger and Daniel Felsenfeld

Library of Congress Cataloging-in-Publication Data

Getzinger, Donna.
  Johann Sebastian Bach and the art of baroque music / Donna Getzinger and
Daniel Felsenfeld.— 1st ed.
    v. cm. — (Classical composers)
  Includes bibliographical references (p. ) and index.
  Contents: A musical education — The organs of Lüneburg — Getting work —
Church music — Dealing with dukes — A time of friendship and love — Classes
and cantatas — The final years — The revival.
  ISBN 1-931798-22-2 (library binding)
  1. Bach, Johann Sebastian, 1685-1750—Juvenile literature. 2. Composers—
Germany—Biography—Juvenile literature. [1. Bach, Johann Sebastian, 1685-
1750. 2. Composers.] I. Felsenfeld, Daniel. II. Title. III. Series.
  ML3930.B2G47 2004
  780'.92—dc22

2003022868

Printed in the United States of America
First Edition

*Thanks to Nancy Bonsall and David Maguire*

# Contents

Johann Sebastian Bach (1685-1750)
*(Courtesy of Museum der Stadt Erfurt-Eberhard Renno.)*

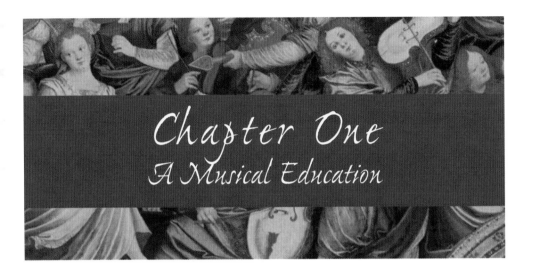

# Chapter One
## A Musical Education

Johann Sebastian Bach was very proud of his children. On a warm spring evening in 1747, he had special reason to be proud of his second oldest son, Carl Philipp Emanuel. Carl, at age thirty-seven, had earned a permanent job in the orchestra of Frederick II, King of Prussia. This young king of the highest court in the land had turned out to be very enlightened when it came to the arts and was a great supporter of advances in musical forms and instruments. Though Bach knew Carl was not paid well enough for his work at the king's court, he was thrilled that his talented son was being appreciated. And he was delighted when Carl invited him to the palace in Potsdam to meet the king.

That night, dressed in his finest breeches, coat, and freshly powdered wig, sixty-two year old Johann

Frederick the Great. *(Courtesy of Rainsville Archive.)*

Sebastian Bach bowed deeply before the king. Over the years Bach had been in many palaces and had seen remarkable displays of the furnishings and decorations of the German nobles. But he had never seen anything quite so grand as this glorious palace. The pure splendor around him made him feel slightly humbled, an odd sensation for the renowned composer, who had spent much of his life daring to challenge dukes and princes.

Bach suspected that he might be asked to play for the king. It was rare that he was not asked to perform when he made an appearance, even if he was only invited as a guest. He didn't know that King Frederick II already had something particularly challenging in mind that evening. Looking around, Bach observed that the empty orchestra platform did not have a harpsichord, but only an early version of a *pianoforte* (the full name of the instrument we refer to as the piano). That was unfortunate for Bach, whose entire career had been devoted to playing the harpsichord or pipe organ. Some people thought these pianofortes would replace harpsichords, but Bach did not agree. He had played a pianoforte once before and did not like the sound it made. While the harpsichord produced a light, delicate sound, the pianoforte he had played made a heavier thunking noise that seemed slightly out of tune to his ear. Rather than worry about it, Bach decided he would play something on the violin instead. He was a virtuoso on that instrument too.

A harpsichord seen from above. The tinny sound produced by the instrument is a typical feature of baroque music. *(Courtesy of Victoria and Albert Museum.)*

But to Bach's delight and surprise, the king sat at the pianoforte and played from memory a piece of music he had written himself. When he was finished, the king asked Bach if he would sit at the piano and try the same piece.

Bach had become a heavy man in his old age. His knees were stiff and his fingers swollen from years of making music. But there was still grace in his movements as he settled onto the bench before the pianoforte and gave the instrument a quick once-over. He plunked a few keys and smiled. It sounded much more pleasant than the one he had played before. The way the hammers hit the wires, instead of plucking them as the harpsichord did, could work to his advantage if he wished to toy with volume. The keys responded easily to his touch, producing a loud sound when he played with force, and a beautifully rounded, quiet tone when he touched them lightly.

After testing the keys, Bach paused a moment to remember the tune of the king's delightful music and then began to play. Improvising, Bach transformed the king's piece before everyone's eyes, and ears, into a gorgeous fugue made of six different intertwining melodies. (Popular in the Baroque era, a fugue involves layers of repeated and intricately overlapping melodies.) When he finished, the king and his court were in awe. Bach accepted their compliments as graciously as he could. It was hard for him to hide his pride behind the humility appropriate for such an occasion.

Bach's music had not always been so well received, however. He had often been criticized for writing music many considered overly complicated. He had quit jobs time and again when his employers could not understand what he had hoped to accomplish with his music. It had been a long career of fighting for what he believed in, and he had rarely won.

By the night in 1747 when he played for Frederick the Great, Bach was an old man. He could only hope his son Carl would have an easier time in his career. Carl had a coveted position at the king's court and should be able to reach the heights of fame that had eluded his father. Three of Bach's other surviving sons also had promising musical careers, and he was glad that his children were living out their adulthoods in these more prosperous times, under an enlightened new ruler, and not in the dim world of his own youth.

Bach was so intrigued by the king's music that he went to his room that night and began to write down the ideas that had come to him so quickly while he improvised for the court. He would call the piece *The Musical Offering* and dedicate it to Frederick the Great. Perhaps the king would be honored; the work might even be published. He would think of that later. For now, as always, he let the music take over, and that night Bach quietly began composing another Baroque masterpiece.

The word baroque comes from an Italian word, *barocco*, meaning bizarre or exuberant. The term is now used to describe the elaborate and emotional style of art, architecture, and music popularized in the seventeenth century. Houses and palaces such as Versailles, near Paris, were built on a grand scale and given magnificently ornate features. Music was intricately styled to be both pleasing to the ear and to reflect what its composers thought was the perfect order of the universe.

However, in the German territories, the splendor of the Baroque age was not so apparent. Central Europe had been ravaged by a war between Catholic and Protestant rulers that lasted from 1618-1648. So much of Germany had been torn apart during the war that wolves and other wild animals had reclaimed some towns. Other towns lost out to the disease and pestilence that came from the polluted water and barren land. The Thirty Years' War, as it came to be known, ended with a peace treaty that kept Germany divided into hundreds of regions run by dukes and their sons, who were princes. These royal lords created the laws, determined what religion would be practiced, and held all the wealth and power in the area they governed.

Many generations of the Bach family had made their home in one of the largest regions of Northern Germany called Thuringia, which was a region divided into several powerful duchies and two principalities. (A duchy is a territory ruled by a duke, while a principality is ruled by a prince.) Thanks to a heavily wooded landscape lush with vegetation, this region's economy was able to rebound sooner than other regions of Germany. The noble lords were able to turn their focus to worldly pleasures. Most nobles in Thuringia had their own court *capelles* (orchestras) made of the finest musicians from all over Europe. A long lineage of Bach men had found that they could make a steady and prosperous living providing musical entertainment for the dukes of this land and the cities they ruled. The people of Thuringia were also fiercely loyal to the Protestant religion they had fought so hard to practice. In this era, music was considered a trade. As with other trades, such as weaving or woodworking, every Bach son was expected to continue working in the family profession.

Johann Sebastian Bach was born on March 21, 1685. He was the eighth child born to Maria Elisabeth and

J. S. Bach grew up in the town of Eisenach. *(After the engraving by Merian, 1650.)*

Ambrosius Bach and one of the four who survived childhood.

All of the Bach sons held the first name of Johann and the second name of another family member. The family tree gets quite confusing with all the Johann Christophs, Johann Jacobs, and Johann Fredrichs. To make it simpler they referred to each other by their middle names. When Bach was born, his parents named him Sebastian after one of his godparents. He became the first Sebastian in the family tree.

In the Bach household, making music was a constant activity. Sebastian began his music studies well before he learned to read and write. Even outside of the Bach family, learning to play an instrument was considered as essential for a child's education as good penmanship. To see a young boy on the way to school without a violin or oboe tucked up under his arm was an unusual sight. Although Ambrosius Bach and his twin brother were both employed as *clavier* musicians (men who played instruments with keyboards), Sebastian began his music studies, as most boys did, on the violin. The violin was a lightweight instrument. Thanks to the handiwork of Italian violin designers such as Antonio Stradivari, it had developed over the last half century into one of the most popular instruments of the era.

Sebastian grew up in Eisenach, a small town rich with history. It was in Eisenach that the founder of the Protestant religion, Martin Luther, had spent his childhood in the sixteenth century. Luther had made it his life's work to protest against the corruption of the Catholic popes and bishops, declaring that Christianity should be based only on what is written in the scriptures and not on how a religious leader interprets the scriptures. When Sebastian turned eight, he began attending the same school where Martin Luther had been a pupil as a

Martin Luther. *(Courtesy of the Library of Congress.)*

The Latin school in Eisenach. Martin Luther studied there in the 1500s, and Johann Sebastian Bach was a pupil in the late seventeenth century. *(Courtesy of Bachhaus, Eisenach.)*

child. Every day, Sebastian walked in the shadow of Wartburg Castle, high on the mountaintop, where Luther had hidden in the year 1521 to translate the Latin Bible into German.

At his famous school, Sebastian learned to read and write in both German and Latin. He also received a thorough education in scripture, which he took quite seriously. Sebastian was a devout Protestant throughout his entire life. The choir for St. George's church was made up of the more talented schoolboys, and because Sebastian had a beautiful soprano singing voice, he became a member.

Music was an important element of Protestant church services. Martin Luther had written hymns in the belief that singing in church was like praying twice. Depending on the size of the church, services could include an organist, a small orchestra, and one or two choirs. A *cantor* was usually hired to teach the choir their songs, and a *capellmeister* directed all the musical activities. None of these musicians worked for free, so the church had to have a large music budget. Sebastian would eventually devote a great deal of his professional life to creating beautiful church music.

The early years of Sebastian's life also instilled in him the importance of family. The Bachs were a tightly knit group. Besides Sebastian's parents, brothers, and sisters, there were always at least three apprentices living with them to trade chores for music lessons from Ambrosius. Various friends and family members frequently stopped by the Bach home for visits. Of all the members of Sebastian's large family, it was his father who mattered the most to him.

It did not take long for Sebastian to master the violin well enough to move on to keyboard instruments. While Sebastian's uncle tutored him on the organ, his father introduced him to the harpsichord. Sebastian must have appreciated this kind of attention from his father, a very busy

The Bach house in Eisenach. *(Courtesy of Langematz.)*

Ambrosius Bach, Johann Sebastian's father. *(Courtesy of Deutsche Staatsbibliothek, Musikabteilung, Berlin.)*

man. Ambrosius Bach was the town piper of Eisenach, a charming job title that meant he was the director of the town's music company. Formal orchestras as we know them today did not exist then; instead, a music company would be made out of whichever musicians were available in a town and whatever instruments those people could play. It was the town piper's job to write or select the music for these random ensembles to play, and to organize performances for every civic event.

Surely Sebastian saw how his father was admired and respected in the community. His various uncles and cousins had similar jobs in other towns, and all were considered among the most valuable people in their communities. All of this served as a constant reminder to young Sebastian that if he practiced very hard, he too could have an important career in music. He might even be hired to work in one of the castles one day, and then he would be surrounded by splendor.

The first nine years of Sebastian's life were apparently happy. Unfortunately, life's ease came to an end when his mother died. Though early and sudden death was fairly common in those days, the loss of Maria Elisabeth was difficult for the whole family. Ambrosius grieved deeply. In addition to his wife's death, Ambrosius's twin brother had also died recently. But even in the midst of his mourning, he knew that he had to take care of the children still living at home.

In order to provide a mother for his children, Ambrosius remarried, taking Barbara Margaretha, the widow of his cousin Johann Günther, as his new bride. She was twice a widow who needed financial help in raising her own two daughters. Sebastian was still nine years old when they were married in November of 1694. The newly rebuilt family had a lovely Christmas together, but tragedy struck shortly afterwards. Ambrosius fell seriously ill, and in February he died, just two days short of his fiftieth birthday and only twelve weeks into his doomed marriage to Margaretha, leaving her widowed a third time.

Margaretha could not take care of all of her stepchildren on her own, so Sebastian and his brother Johann

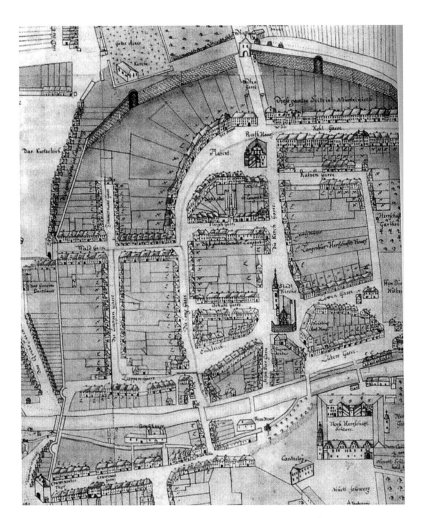

An early eighteenth-century map of Ohrdruf.

Jacob were sent to Ohrdruf to be raised by their oldest surviving brother, Johann Christoph. Sebastian had never known Christoph well because there was a fourteen-year age difference between them. The year Sebastian was born, Christoph had left home to start his career as an apprentice to one of the most revered composers in the land, Johann Pachelbel. As an apprentice, Christoph helped Pachelbel by doing tasks for him and in return was given advanced instruction in music. This work included everything from copying out orchestral parts from the master's handwritten scores, recopying music to study, and writing rudimentary musical exercises and compositions. Christoph also cleaned up after livestock and mended clothes. All in all, it was an honorable and much envied position for a boy his age.

After his apprenticeship with Pachelbel, Christoph had become a much-desired organist. At the age of eighteen, he had accepted a post rarely offered to musicians so young: that of organist at St. Michael's, the principal church in Ohrdruf. St. Michael's had two organs, one of them of a considerable size. Unfortunately, Christoph soon found out the larger of the organs needed too many repairs to be playable, and it would take another ten years before the repairs were finished. Christoph had to make do with the smaller, less impressive organ. In 1695, his position as organist in the village of Ohrdruf paid him well enough in money, food, and wood (in those days a salary might include household necessities) to be able to start a family. He had only recently married Dorothea von Hof, daughter of the town clerk, when he agreed to take his young, parentless brothers, Sebastian and Jacob, into his home.

The only problem now for Sebastian and Jacob was how they would get to Ohrdruf, thirty miles away from Eisenach, in the freezing March weather. None of their surviving adult relatives had the time to take them by horse or wagon through the snowy and muddy route. So the two boys, ages ten and thirteen, had no choice but to slog the whole way on foot, carrying everything they owned on their backs.

Fortunately, Christoph turned out to be a great older brother. He gave Sebastian private lessons on the harpsichord, organ, and fiddle. He also taught Sebastian a little about how music was written for keyboard instruments. To do this, Christoph put Sebastian to work copying organ and harpsichord music written by German composers such as Johann Caspar Kerll, Jakob Forberger, and Pachelbel. Sebastian enjoyed this activ-

Title page of Johann Pachelbel's *Hexachordum Apollinis.* *(Courtesy of British Museum.)*

ity and eagerly pored over the manuscripts. There were some manuscripts, however, that he was not allowed to touch. Christoph kept his most prized collections under lock and key in his study. Legend has it that Sebastian desired so much to see these forbidden pages of music that he would sneak behind his brother's back to do so. Over a period of six months Sebastian would wake in the middle of the night, slip into the study, and pull out these precious manuscripts. Sitting by the window, able to see only by the light of the moon, he painstakingly copied these scores for his own personal use. For Sebastian, seeing the written notes spread out on paper and studying the way music looked as well as sounded gave him inspiration. He realized he wanted to be a composer.

Ohrdruf was a small town with a growing marketplace that had been founded by Scottish-Irish monks in the year 727. It had few attractions except for its prestigious private boys' academy. Parents from all over the area sent their sons to this school. At first it didn't look as though Sebastian would be able to attend; the tuition was too expensive for Christoph's budget. Luckily, some scholarship money had been set aside for gifted students with little money, and Sebastian and Jacob were permitted to take classes. Jacob studied at the academy for only one year before quitting to return to Eisenach as an apprentice to the man who had filled his father's position as town piper. Sebastian, meanwhile, continued to learn Latin, Greek, and of course, music.

Sebastian completed eight years of schooling in only

four, rising to the top of his class, and neared graduation at the age of fifteen instead of the usual nineteen. This kind of academic performance was unprecedented in Bach men, most of whom were certainly talented musically but not intellectuals. Many of them barely made it through school at all. Unfortunately, as Sebastian neared graduation, the scholarship money ran out. During the years he had been attending school and living with his brother, his sister-in-law had given birth to three sons. Fifteen-year-old Sebastian knew that Christoph didn't earn enough money to feed his family of five, and Christoph had never been able to afford to pay the high tuition for Sebastian's school.

At the age of fifteen, most members of the Bach family had quit school to become apprentices, opting to make their way in the professional music world. Any Bach with talent could get good work in Germany as a musician without a degree, so known and respected was their name. Higher education was really only for those who wanted teaching positions at academies or universities. Christoph urged his younger brother to follow in the family footsteps, as he had done, by apprenticing, which would get Sebastian out of the house and earning a little income. But Sebastian did not feel apprenticing was the right direction for him. If he could find a way to pay for it, he wanted to graduate from school and get one of the higher-level jobs that extra education could win for him.

Until he could figure out how to achieve his goals,

Sebastian searched for a way to bring in some money to the family. Still blessed with a beautiful singing voice, he became a member of the church choir and earned a few pennies a week. The choristers were also allowed to sing in the streets, a practice called *currende*, for extra coins. This was not nearly enough money for tuition, however, so the director of the church choir, Elias Herda, convinced Sebastian to go north to Lüneburg and audition for a job singing in the St. Michael's monastery. The monastery had quite a bit of wealth and paid their choristers very well. In addition, the monastery provided the talented boys a place to live and an education at no cost. This sounded like the perfect arrangement to Sebastian, so in the spring of 1700 he convinced a friend named Georg Erdmann to quit school in Ohrdruf and join him on the one-hundred-eighty-mile hike north to an uncertain destiny.

# Chapter Two
## The Organs of Lüneburg

Nothing about Lüneburg was familiar to Sebastian. It was four times the size of Ohrdruf and very near Hamburg, which was the largest city in all of Germany. Over ten thousand people lived in this important salt-trading town, the halfway mark between Hamburg and Hanover. Lüneburg was part of the Brunswick-Lüneburg duchy. Frederick William I, the Great Elector of the Holy Roman Empire, ruled over it from afar. But the biggest difference for Sebastian was the fact that the Bach name had no significance for the people in Lüneburg. Bach musicians had rarely come this far north. Any success he had would be on his own merit and not based on the family reputation. Although this made auditioning more daunting, Sebastian Bach relished the challenge.

Sebastian knew he would have no problem getting

employed—if he had been at all doubtful, he would have probably followed his brother's advice and stayed in Ohrdruf or Eisenach. The welcome reception his fine soprano voice was given at St. Michael's monastery proved Sebastian correct: he and Georg were hired right away. No doubt their former choir director had sent word that the boys were coming, and that may have helped them to get work so quickly. Timing may also have been part of their good fortune, as the boys arrived just before Easter, when the demands upon church musicians were at the heaviest. But it was talent alone that got Sebastian and Georg hired into the select ensemble at the St. Michael's school, the Mattins Choir, which boasted a

The town of Lüneburg. (Engraving from Merian's *Topographia,* 1654, courtesy of Bachhaus, Eisenach.)

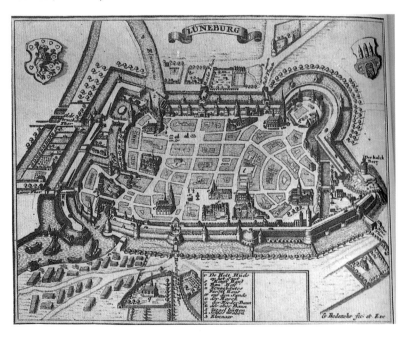

wonderful sound. To Sebastian's delight, he was paid third highest of the choristers.

The St. Michael's school was over two hundred and fifty years old. The monastery, another four hundred years older than the school, had been a Catholic church and monastery until the Protestant reformation of the 1500s, when it was transformed into a secondary school for boys.

The fifteen members of the Mattins Choir had plenty of work to keep them busy between their studies. They had to perform at every church function, which included Saturday vespers and Sunday main services, as well as on feast days and special occasions like weddings and funerals. They sang all of the difficult concert pieces, usually just after the minister's sermon, while the ordinary choir sang only hymns and chants. It was a wonderful experience for Sebastian. But soon after arriving, he feared it might end too quickly. Only a few months after arriving in Lüneburg, puberty set in, and with it Sebastian's voice began to change. He lost his beautiful, high singing range.

At first he tried to hide the awful cracking sounds his voice made. He kept quiet for eight whole days, not even speaking in a whisper. But eventually the secret came out. Sebastian's voice had gone quickly from high soprano to deep baritone, and there was no way to hide it. He was lucky, however: it turned out that the St. Michael's school had a shortage of good bass singers, so they kept him on.

An interior view of St. Michael's Church, as depicted in this eighteenth-century painting by Joachim Burmester. *(Courtesy of Heimat Museum, Lüneburg.)*

The music the boys were required to sing was *poly-phonic*, meaning it had a multi-textured sound, with more than one line sung at the same time. Imagine two melodies, both beautiful on their own, but played simultaneously to an even more beautiful musical effect. This technique is called *counterpoint* and continues to be one of the first things an aspiring composer learns. Bach's teachers never took the time to explain the intricacies of how polyphonic music was composed because the job of composing was ranked very low in the hierarchy of musical professions. Still, young Sebastian had a natural curiosity about music and felt compelled to study how it was made. Using his amazing ears, he began to reason out the mathematically complex rules governing this type of music.

The world today knows Bach as a great composer, but unlike the prodigies who would follow, such as Mozart, Beethoven, and Mendelssohn, Bach did not begin to compose until late in his teenage years. At this time, he was still studying how other composers worked and not yet experimenting with his own ideas. His brother, Christoph, had taught him to read music manuscripts and had provided him with plenty of opportunities to copy music. Sebastian kept at this hobby once he moved into the St. Michael's dormitory in order to privately advance his skills. He had to do this secretly, under the cover of night, as he had done in his brother's home.

Sebastian would wait until all the others in his rooming house had fallen asleep, and then sneak down to the library. He would drag a huge book from the shelf, open the volume and find a table near a window. Just as he had back at Christoph's house, Sebastian worked by the light of the moon. With a previously prepared goose quill pen and handmade music paper, Sebastian began his copying work for the night. Then he had to cover his tracks, sneak back to his room, and hope nobody noticed his weary eyes in the morning. Few would have understood his passion for discovering the methods of composition, and keeping his actions private kept him from having to defend himself against his teachers' criticisms.

While Sebastian got into St. Michael's because of his singing, those at the school began noticing that he had another, even greater, talent. Sebastian had brought his violin with him to Lüneburg and put it to good use, occasionally accompanying the choir as they sang. By the time he turned sixteen he was also helping out when

he could by playing a variety of the other instruments his father had taught him. Having shown advanced skill at the harpsichord, he was invited to learn to play the organ. He was no stranger to

With great enthusiasm, Bach learned to play the organ, an instrument many of his relatives before him had played. *(Courtesy of Archiv für Kunst and Geschichte.)*

this instrument, given that both his uncle and older brother were organists, but now he devoted himself to it as much as he could. Bach loved to get his feet on the pedals, his fingers on the two separate keyboards, and to make the huge pipes sound. He learned quickly, and soon he was playing in church for a number of performances. Every now and then he was even allowed to substitute for the official organist.

In 1701, Sebastian's second summer in Lüneburg, a well-known builder of pipe organs, Johann Balthasar Held, came to fix the instrument at St. Michael's Church, by far the largest organ Sebastian had seen to date. Ever curious and wanting to expand his knowledge of the organ, Sebastian spent as much time with Held as he could in order to learn about how these massive instruments were put together.

A pipe organ is such a large instrument that churches have special lofts built just to hold them, and the organist playing the instrument can barely be seen beneath the massive steel pipes. Imagine giant flutes standing on end atop a box fifty feet wide by thirty feet deep and full of air, called the wind box. Giant bellows push the air through it and up into the pipes to produce the organ's rich, full sound. These bellows are so large that a person would be hired to walk back and forth on them to help squeeze out the air while the organist played.

The first organs were invented in ancient Greece. Water pressure was used to get the wind into the pipes and the sound was loud and unreliable. Armies of the

The elaborate organ in St. John's Church, in Lüneburg. *(Courtesy of Pierre Vallaton, Organa Europe.)*

Roman Empire discovered that the loud and unruly organ made a good weapon for scaring enemies during war. Tabletop versions of a much nicer-sounding organ were slowly introduced into churches during the Middle Ages. After Martin Luther introduced his hymnals to the Protestant church services, the organ became a mandatory part of church construction.

There are sixty-one keys on a manual, or keyboard, and there is one pipe for each key. Often an organ will have two to four manuals for the organist's hands and another for his feet. The size of the pipe determines its sound—the smaller the pipe, the higher the pitch. To change the sound of all those pipes and keys, an organist will apply stops, which are mechanisms that control the amount of air that goes into the pipes. To let up on a stop, a little knob must be pulled out of the wall. This is the origin of the phrase "pulling out all the stops." Through a combination of stops and pipes, the organist can make one instrument sound like an entire orchestra. No two organs are identical, which makes playing an unfamiliar one a challenge, even for the most talented performer.

While Sebastian was still a student, he wanted to get as much experience on the organ as he could. Sometimes this meant hours of sitting and watching repairs being made. At other times, once the organ was ready to be played again, Sebastian would have to pay a bellows operator so he could practice between church events. Over the two years that Sebastian spent in Lüneburg, all of the organists in town got to know him and were intrigued by his enthusiasm for their work and his natural ability at their chosen instrument. They were glad to give Sebastian lessons if he would do a chore or two for them in exchange. Georg Böhm, the organist at St. John's Church, the largest church in Lüneburg, particularly took a liking to Sebastian. Böhm had been taught to play by the famous Hamburg organist J. Adam Reinken.

Bach never had a great teacher. Instead, he cobbled together his learning every way he could. He soaked up knowledge from the local organists and studied the

Johann Adam Reinken at the keyboard, with two other major seventeenth-century German musicians, Johann Thiele and Dietrich Buxtehude. *(Courtesy of Museum für Hamburgische Geschichte.)*

manuscripts of composers beyond his geographical ken. Perhaps because of the pieced together nature of Bach's musical education and the lack of a single mentor, he developed a style that showed the influences of many of his contemporaries. Even as he learned from the men around him, Bach was beginning to make his own kind of music. But when, later, he encountered the music of the Italians, specifically Antonio Vivaldi, Bach's style would change completely.

During this time, however, Bach was still apprenticing himself to the masters he knew. Since Bach had a cousin living in Hamburg, he probably traveled there and was able to see Reinken play the organ at St. Catherine's Church. This was the largest and most beautiful organ in all of Northern Germany. Bach never forgot this instrument. Later in life he would tell his children and students about it, letting them know that he "could not praise the beauty and variety of these reeds highly enough."

When not listening to or reading organ music, Bach worked hard at transcribing and modifying scores. He might take a piece written for one instrument—say, the violin or the harpsichord—and then re-write it so it could be played on a different instrument. Transcription is difficult but invaluable as a learning tool since a transcriber must be patient, have an awareness of the capabilities of various instruments, and be able to hear the different possibilities for a melody.

As Bach neared graduation from St. Michael's school in 1702, at the age of seventeen, he found himself in a quandary over what to do with his life. He could go to Hamburg as an apprentice to the great organist Reinken, but the revered master was beginning to turn his interest to writing operas instead of

George Frideric Handel. *(Courtesy of Covent Garden Archives, Royal Opera House.)*

organ music. Other students were already flocking to Reinken's door to be a part of this experience—one of those young men was George Frideric Handel, who was born the same year as Sebastian Bach and was on the verge of becoming an internationally famous composer. It could have been a great opportunity for Sebastian, too, but he was not raised to appreciate opera, and had little interest in trying his hand at it.

Sebastian considered sticking it out, graduating from St. Michael's, and going on to a university to earn an advanced degree. It would be expensive, but he was certain he could get a scholarship, as he had for secondary school. But the more he thought about it, he realized that his heart was not in that choice either. He felt that he had learned enough at this point to begin making his mark on the musical world.

Ultimately, Sebastian Bach decided it was high time that he begin his professional career. He dropped out of school, left Lüneburg, and headed back to the familiar landscape of Thuringia to put his education and well-known surname to good use.

# Chapter Three
## Getting Work

Johann Sebastian Bach was uniquely talented when he left school, and he had already gained quite a bit of experience at the organ to make him employable. That did not mean, however, that jobs came easily to him. He had to audition just like any other musician seeking work, and because of his youth, seventeen-year-old Bach was judged more critically than most adults.

Hearing that there was an opportunity at the Ducal Court in Celle, thirty miles south of Lüneburg, Bach decided he would go there first in his quest for employment. Common folk were not permitted inside the castles of nobility without invitation, but the Duke of Celle seemed to have an affinity for students and musicians, so Bach was not turned away when he showed up at the castle gates wearing his uniform from the academy and holding a letter of introduction from one of his teachers.

The Celle castle was unlike any building Bach had ever been inside. Though built according to German tastes, the decoration was distinctly French, a style unfamiliar to the straight-laced German folk. The Duke of Celle had traveled to France and desired to have his own home resemble the grand palace that was home to the extravagant King Louis XIV. Therefore, Celle was known as "little Versailles" for its lavishness and excesses. The band that the Duke kept under his employ was made up mostly of French musicians, so during the time that Bach spent at Celle auditioning, he got a solid taste of the more ornamental sounding French music.

As with Italian music, French music was far more fanciful than German. King Louis XIV (who ruled in France from 1661-1715) considered music so important

The castle at Celle.

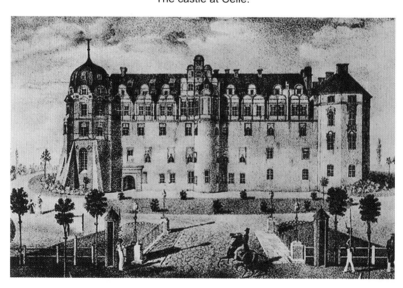

that he started the first dance academy and put together the largest orchestra of string instruments in the world. French instrumental music focused a good deal on purely entertaining forms such as the overture (an introduction to an opera) and the suite (a combina-

Louis XIV, of France. *(Courtesy of Château de Versailles.)*

tion of slow and fast dances). This was quite a different approach than that of the sterner Germans, who preferred their music to have purpose. Bach found the beauty in the music of both cultures, and worked out his own adaptation of these various styles—particularly later in his life, when he would write a set of keyboard pieces called the *French Suites*.

The Duke of Celle opted not to hire Bach for a permanent position, but Bach had already heard of another job opening, this time back in Thuringia, in a town called Sangerhausen. When musicians found good jobs they usually stuck with them for life. All too often they had to wait for an organist or town piper to die before they could improve their job prospects. In the case of Sangerhausen, Bach got word that the organist of St. Jacob's Church had recently been buried, in July 1702. Considering that organ music was Bach's passion (much more so than fiddling with foreign tunes or operas) he wasted no time making the two-hundred-mile trek on foot to this small town near where he grew up.

He must have given an excellent audition. The town council voted unanimously that Bach should take over the job as principal organist and slated him to start working in November of that year. Unfortunately, Duke Johann Georg of Saxe-Weissenfels, who ruled over Sangerhausen, intervened. No matter how talented Bach may have been, the duke believed Bach was too young and inexperienced. He wanted to give the job to an older man named Augustin Kobelius, who had already proven himself elsewhere. The duke's interference with their decision infuriated the town council, who felt they should have been able to make the selection on their own, but there was nothing they could do to change the outcome. This rejection was a big blow for Bach as well, but he kept his head high and went looking for work again.

Bach finally found a job in January of 1703. He was hired to be part of the capelle for Duke Johann Ernst at the court of Weimar. Word had gotten around that there was a young talented member of the Bach family roaming around looking for suitable employment. Sebastian Bach's grandfather had served the Weimar court sixty years before, so the Bach name was well loved and respected there. To earn his salary, Sebastian had to play a variety of instruments, including the violin and harpsichord. He played both sacred (religious) and secular (non-religious) music.

Bach's official position at Weimer was that of "lackey."

This meant that in addition to playing music he had to do chores and serve as a valet. Although his status was lowly, his skills on the organ were very well respected. Bach was often called upon to substitute for the court's organist, Johann Effler, who was fairly old and not always well. While this was an honor, Bach's time at Weimer was merely a brief stop on his journey to find a post of his own.

Bach only stayed in Weimar for six months. He moved on quickly because exciting things were happening in the nearby town of Arnstadt. The organ at the New Church (so named after the original church burned to the ground and had to be rebuilt) had been going through repairs for two years and now it was almost finished. The town council of Arnstadt wanted to have it inspected and throw a big celebration to inaugurate it. Arnstadt was another town in which many men with the Bach name had been employed over the years, including Bach's own father, and the council was interested in meeting this new young Bach who had played the organ at St. Michael's in Lüneburg and had so thoroughly impressed the people of Sangerhausen. Sebastian Bach may have only been eighteen years old at the time, but he already had a reputation for being the most knowledgeable organist in Thuringia.

Bach was invited to come to Arnstadt to examine their great organ. They spared no cost to get him there, paying for a private coach to carry him and giving him an honorarium for the examination, plus extra money for

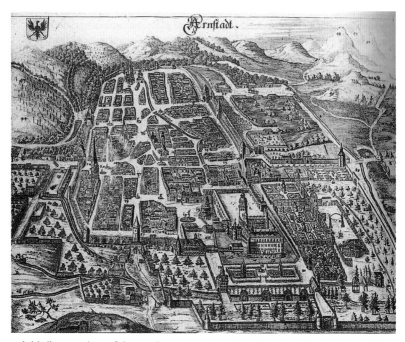

A bird's-eye-view of Arnstadt. *(Engraving by Pius Rösel von Rosenhoff, c.1700.)*

food and expenses. This was by far the best treatment Bach had ever received, and he felt like nobility. After Bach gave his nod of approval to the instrument, the town council then invited Bach to play the organ at the special dedication recital scheduled for July 8, 1703. Clearly, Bach had proven to these people that he could more than meet their expectations.

But this was not all that Arnstadt offered him. It was decided, after the dedication ceremony, that Bach should stay in Arnstadt and replace the current organist at the New Church. Andrea Börner had been the organist throughout the repairs, and he fully expected he would maintain the post once the instrument was ready for use.

As the repairs took longer than expected to complete, Börner became impatient and difficult. This may have been part of the reason that the town council chose to replace him. Bach, however, did not feel right about forcing Börner out of his job, so he suggested that Börner stay on to play the early Sunday services at full pay. Of course he knew that the church budget could not be stretched to pay two organists, so he took a risk that the council considered him valuable enough to find another way to cover his salary. He was right to be so self-assured. The town agreed to this plan and arranged to pay Bach's salary by taking contributions from wealthy town members who did not want to lose the bright young man. Bach wound up earning four times as much as anyone who had ever filled this post. Börner soon transferred to another church in the city.

Bach was in an enviable position. He had a job with high status and low workload. He only had to write and play preludes and postludes at a few services, maybe three a week, with extra performances on major holidays. In his spare time he joined the local instrumental ensemble as a violinist and sometimes entertained at the castle of Count Anton Günther. There was only one problem: Bach had to teach the boys' choir and instrumental ensemble at the local secondary school.

Bach had never been interested in teaching, but he might have liked this job if the boys had been talented and well-behaved the way he and his friends at St. Michael's had been. Unfortunately, these Arnstadt boys

The New Church of Arnstadt's grand interior and organ. *(Courtesy of Evangelisch-lutherisches, Ohrdurf.)*

were not a diligent, pious, or particularly talented lot. They were mostly children of wealthy and accomplished tradesmen, who knew what they could get away with and pushed the limits constantly. They were in no hurry to graduate, as they did not need to work to support themselves, and many of them were already in their early twenties while Bach was still only eighteen.

Never one to settle for mediocrity, Bach decided to whip this choir into shape and bring forth great musicality from them. The perfectionist side of him came out, and he made large demands on his students. He refused to accept sloppy singing, something the boys had got away with in the past. He treated them all as lazy children, talking down to them and demeaning them when they made mistakes, which made the students angry. What had started out as an extra-curricular activity they took part in to pass time had suddenly become an obligation—and an annoying one at that. Bach may have wanted them to be a prize-winning chorus, but they rebelled against his constant hammering.

The tension came to a head when Bach encountered six of his students near the marketplace on his way home from a rehearsal with the court orchestra at Count Günther's castle. The boys had sticks in their hands and were ready to attack. During class that afternoon Bach had called a boy named Geyersbach a nanny-goat because his bassoon playing was so miserably bad. Geyersbach was not too happy about it. The six young men blocked Bach's path. Geyersbach called Bach a "dirty dog" and struck out at him. Luckily, part of the formal outfit that Bach had been wearing that day for his appearance at the castle included a sword slung at his side. He drew it as the gang descended on him. The students had not counted on Bach striking back. In fear for their own lives, they turned on their heels and ran.

Bach and the bassoon player were called before the school authorities and made to explain their behavior. Bach was reprimanded for his name-calling and told "he must get along with the students, and that they must not make each other's lives miserable." Bach was not happy with this response since his contract stipulated his duties were to "appear promptly on Sundays, feast days, and other days of public divine service in the said New Church at the organ entrusted to you; to play the latter as is fitting; to keep a watchful eye over it and take faithful care of it." Nothing in these lines suggested he would be saddled with the responsibility of reluctant or even antagonistic students.

Problems between Bach and his students continued through the next year. But Bach created more friction with the school authorities on his own. They granted him a leave of absence to travel to Lübeck to see a performance by Dietrich Buxtehude, an internationally famous organist and composer, and a peer of Reinken. The two hundred-mile journey would take a considerable amount of time, so Bach was awarded a month's leave of absence to improve his knowledge of his art.

Bach arrived in Lübeck in November 1705, just in time to see Buxtehude play a series of concerts for the Christmas season. Enthralled with Buxtehude's inventive organ playing, Bach ignored his scheduled return date and stayed well past the New Year in order to soak up as much of this music as possible. To pay for his extended time in Lübeck, Bach got work in Buxtehude's orchestra, most likely playing either violin or harpsichord. He did not return to Arnstadt until February. This neglect angered the council members, even though Bach had appointed one of his very capable cousins to substitute for him while he was away. The council reprimanded Bach, but he felt no guilt about his actions, stating only that he had "…hoped the organ playing had been so well taken care of by the one he had engaged for the purpose that no complaint could be entered on that account."

Frustrated by Bach's glib attitude, the council then

attacked him for the new music he had been composing and playing in church since he had returned. Although Bach had put together a wonderful orchestra of trumpets, strings, and drums, his efforts were not at all appreciated. They council accused him of "...having hitherto made many curious *variationes* in the chorale, and mingled many strange tones in it, and for the fact that the congregation has been confused by it." Bach had been playing around with some polyphony in his preludes, having learned a few new musical tricks from Buxtehude, but Arnstadt did not like the changes. They wanted their music plain, simple, and easy to follow.

Dietrich Buxtehude was a prolific composer. His music, as well as his deft organ playing, had tremendous influence on Bach's work. *(Courtesy of Museum für Hamburgische Geschichte.)*

It is important to remember that church music was the only music most common people came into contact with, unless they could play at home. There was little in the way of live entertainment available to them. All week people looked forward to hearing the organ and chorus, and what they heard was much discussed. No matter how eager they were to hear music, though, the people did not particularly care to hear unfamiliar music. Certain familiar sounds were both expected and desired. When the music strayed from what they were used to, the churchgoers would inevitably get upset.

Between Bach's antagonistic relationships with his students, his defiance of the school's orders, and the new music he was producing, the council had had enough. By November 1706, the council of Arnstadt was totally fed up with Bach's antics. They told him point blank that "he must not be ashamed to make music with the students" if he wanted to stay in their employ. On top of that, they reprimanded him for inviting a woman to sing in the organ loft. Women were expressly forbidden to sing in a German Protestant church, and for Bach to invite one to do so was a grave error in judgment. The woman was most likely his cousin, nineteen-year-old Maria Barbara, with whom he was falling in love and would eventually marry.

Things were obviously not going well in Arnstadt, so Bach kept his eyes and ears open for new employment. The ongoing antagonism over what kind of music was considered acceptable made him all the more passionate about composing complicated pieces. Throughout the rest of his life, Bach would retain this defiant, rebellious streak. He knew that he'd be able to get his compositions performed eventually, for he no longer had any intention of spending his life as the organist for the New Church in Arnstadt.

While in Lübeck, Bach had been exposed to a form of vocal music he had never heard before. Buxtehude had composed *cantatas,* works similar to operas. Both usually have a choir, a small ensemble of instruments, and vocal soloists. Unlike an opera, however, a cantata is performed without

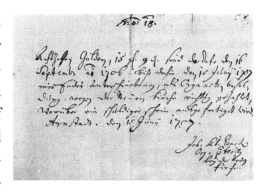

A receipt for Bach's salary as organist in Arnstadt. *(Courtesy of Rainsville Archive.)*

scenery, costumes, or being staged. Also, cantatas tend to be about biblical stories, whereas operas are theatrical melodramas. Bach began to experiment with writing his own cantatas while in Arnstadt, and these early compositions are noteworthy for their liveliness and vigor.

The style of music Bach is better known for is the fugue. A fugue is a complicated musical form in which a composer writes a short melody that repeats while variations on that melody play over and underneath it. Fugues can be incredibly complex. It was this densely layered, intricately structured music the people of Arnstadt so disliked.

Twenty-one-year-old Bach needed to find a more hospitable environment for his new music. In December of 1706 Bach learned that J. Georg Ahle, the organist of St. Blasius's Church in Mühlhausen, had died. Ahle, together with his father, had held this position for more than fifty years. Because of this, the people of

Mühlhausen wanted a highly respected professional organist to take his place. They wanted someone not just competent, but exceptional. They invited Johann Sebastian Bach to audition.

Bach requested a leave of absence from the town council of Arnstadt in order to travel the thirty-six miles to Mühlhausen to audition on Easter Sunday. No doubt the town council was displeased with the fact that Bach was again going to disappear during a major holiday when his services were needed most. At the same time, however, the ill will between Bach and the town council of Arnstadt might have been why they permitted it. If Bach left his post at the New Church, the council would be free to find a new organist with a temperament better suited to their own.

Bach had been well prepared for his audition. Knowing that they had a fondness for vocal music at St. Blasius's, he had prepared an Easter cantata and a hymn that consisted of many movements. In addition, he provided them with an instrumental piece called a *sinfonia,* which in the eighteenth century was a composition similar to a sonata. Bach gave the audition the best he had to offer. While the town council of Mühlhausen had reservations about hiring a musician who had such a difficult time getting along at his previous post, they were finally won over by the quality of his musicianship. It was time, again, for Bach to move on.

# Chapter Four
## Church Music

During the summer of 1707, Bach made his way to Mühlhausen, the second largest city in Thuringia. As he approached the city, he must have been impressed by the skyline of thirteen tall church spires amid large modern buildings, all corralled by a city wall that had been built nearly four hundred years earlier. His mood was surely light as he came through the city gates, because he knew that the politics of this city were vastly different from those of the small town where he had just spent four long years.

Mühlhausen was an independent city. No prince reigned over it, and the elected council members and *burgomasters* (mayors) got their orders directly from Emperor Joseph I in far away Vienna. Because of its size and political freedom, Mühlhausen resembled the great

The city of Mühlhausen, the second largest in the region of Thuringia.

northern cities of Hamburg and Lübeck. Bach liked this aspect of his new home very much. Mostly he liked the fact that, unlike Arnstadt, its religious leaders did not control the town. In fact, a delicate balance of power existed between the elected politicians and the church officials. Issues involving the town were divided into either public matters or religious matters. They even went so far as to have different meeting places. The city council met at St. Mary's Church, and the head of the church government gathered at St. Blasius's Church.

Another thing that Bach liked about Mühlhausen was that none of his relatives had worked there. He would have to earn the respect of his employers on his own. He always preferred to stand on his own talent and ability.

In addition to being church organist, Bach also became the unofficial town music director. He was never given the title, but he definitely organized all the major musical events in the town. For all his effort Bach was going to receive the same salary as he had in Arnstadt. He would be paid eighty-five guilders (about forty dollars) a year plus the benefits of wood, corn, fish and the free transportation of his belongings from Arnstadt.

Now Bach earned enough money and had enough status as a musician to feel comfortable about starting a family. A musician wasn't considered a master until he was married with children, so it was time for this twenty-two year old man to get his personal life in order.

Bach had met the woman he would marry in Arnstadt. Maria Barbara was a distant relation, the daughter of his father's cousin. When she arrived in Arnstadt in 1704 she had just been orphaned at the age of twenty. She came to live with her aunt and, while there, got to know Sebastian. The two fell deeply in love. Up until this point Bach had been solely interested in his own pursuits of music and the best job opportunity, but it was with Maria Barbara that Bach's belief in the importance of love and family began to develop. When Bach was in Lübeck, Buxtehude had given him the chance to inherit the highly revered position of town organist when he re-tired, on the condition that Bach marry his daughter. But Bach was already in love with Maria Barbara and could not convince himself to turn away from his heart's desire just to acquire a job, no matter how prestigious.

With his new situation in Mühlhausen, everything changed. Soon after getting this great post, Bach also inherited fifty guilders from an uncle who had died over the summer. The unexpected extra money cinched the deal, and the wedding was scheduled for October 17, 1707.

There was no honeymoon for the young couple. Bach had many duties to perform in Mühlhausen, such as leading the town ensembles, teaching both the church and school choirs, and even teaching the choir at St. Mary and Magdalen's School for girls. The workload was so heavy that Bach hired two assistants to help him. In return for their dedication, Bach gave them private music lessons. He did not, apparently, encounter any substantial difficulties with his Mühlhausen students. No record exists of any complaint by or against him.

The composing efforts that Arnstadt had so frowned upon were appreciated in Bach's new home. In fact, he wrote a special cantata to honor two of the newly elected city council members in February of 1708. He called it his "little council piece," which was a great understatement. The people of Mühlhausen had never heard music as exciting and unique as this new work by Bach. They were so thrilled by it that they put up the money to have the work engraved in copper so that printed copies could be made. It was officially titled the "Congratulatory Church Motet."

This was the first time his work was published. In his lifetime, most of his work would never go to press, and this piece bears the distinction of being one of the most widely celebrated until long after his death. It is interesting to note that this cantata was published well before any works by Handel or Georg Philipp Telemann, although both of those composers, unlike Bach, became internationally famous in their own lifetimes.

But the teaching and composing were side jobs. Most of Bach's time was spent playing the giant organ at St. Blasius's Church. This church had been built early in the thirteenth century. The first organ for the church was installed in 1560. Mühlhausen's organ builder, Wender, had spent four years rebuilding the ancient instrument just before the turn of the century. All the same, by the time Bach got his hands on the instrument less than twenty years later, he felt the organ needed even more repairs. After making a long, detailed list of what was required, he presented his ideas to the

Cantata No. 71, Bach's first printed composition. *(Courtesy of British Library.)*

church officials. It is a sign of the respect Bach's expertise commanded that his requests were immediately approved. He gave his designs to Wender, and the two of them went to work rebuilding the organ.

Mühlhausen had been one of the last places in Northern Germany to fully adopt Protestantism. For that reason two distinct camps of believers existed within the city walls with very different points of view about the proper way to worship God. One sect was known as the Pietists, who felt that life should be devoid of worldly pleasures (anything that would detract one's attention from the goal of preparing one's soul for heaven). The

Pietists did not allow music to be played anywhere except church services, and even there the music had to be very pure and simple—the organ playing was only to accompany the singing of hymns. The ornate music Bach composed was considered to be self-indulgent and therefore disrespectful to God. This was difficult for Bach to understand, for he considered his music to be his highest form of tribute to God.

The second group of worshippers was known as the Orthodox sect. The people who preferred this more relaxed view toward religion tended to be wealthier, and surely part of the reason they were more willing to embellish their services with organ music, choirs, and orchestras was because they could afford it. The Orthodox believers enjoyed their entertainments, but they did set limits. Music and theater had to be either for the

Another view of Mühlhausen's spire-filled skyline. *(Courtesy of Museum am Linden bühl, Mühlhausen.)*

church or for the concert hall. Anything created purely for personal enjoyment was sinful.

Mühlhausen was not the only place in Germany where the conflict between these two views of the Protestant faith existed, but the arguments here were fierce. Bach was often pulled into the conflict because he was not only the highest-ranking musician in town but had a tendency to write music that seemed to show off his musical abilities. Bach himself was deeply religious, but he detested political conflict and refused to take sides. He just wanted to write and play music—and to do it his way, without interference. The constant bickering wore on his nerves, and though he did not purposely seek out another place of employment, he knew that if something better came along he would not hesitate to leave.

Something better did come his way in June of 1708. Duke Wilhelm Ernst of Weimar invited Bach to his court to have a look at his church organ. The instrument was going through renovations, and Bach now had a reputation for being the best man to inspect organ repairs. While Bach was in Weimar the court organist Johann Effler decided to retire, claiming his health was failing in his old age. The post was offered to Bach.

The supportive people of Mühlhausen deserved an explanation for Bach's resignation after only a year of service. On June 25, Bach wrote a heartfelt letter requesting his dismissal. It is the earliest document written in his hand to survive. He starts by flattering those he is about to disappoint by addressing his letter to "Your

Magnificence, Honored and Noble Sirs, Honored and Learned Sirs, Honored and Wise Sirs, Most Gracious Patroni and Gentlemen." The letter went on to explain that "…however simple my manner of living, I can live but poorly considering the house rent and other most necessary expenses. Now, God has brought it to pass that an unexpected change should offer itself to me, in which I see the possibility of a more adequate living…"

Bach must have felt guilty about leaving so abruptly, especially after having just started the massive work on the organ, so he added that if there was anything more needed of him, he would happily comply. The town council and church officials took him up on that offer. For the next two years he was asked to write and perform for the election ceremonies, and he was invited to come to Mühlhausen to check on the progress of the organ until it was completed. One final favor was to find a successor to the post of organist at St. Blasius's Church. Bach introduced his cousin, J. Friederich Bach to them, and he was hired without question (though his pay was considerably less than Sebastian's had been).

In 1708, right after the still-newlywed couple arrived in Weimar, Maria Barbara gave birth to the first of Bach's twenty children, Catharina Dorothea. Bach and Maria Barbara would have five other children while living in Weimar. Of them, Wilhelm Friedemann, Carl Philipp Emanuel, and Johann Gottfried would go on to be musicians; the twins Maria Sophia and Johann Christoph would not live out their first month.

# Chapter Five
## Dealing with Dukes

Bach and his wife left the bustling metropolis behind and moved to Weimar, a small town of only five thousand inhabitants. What Weimar lacked in size, however, it made up for in culture. This was due, for the most part, to one of the co-regents who ruled over this land, Duke Wilhelm Ernst.

The Duke's father had died in 1683, and at that point Wilhelm Ernst and his brother had split the duchy. Wilhelm Ernst, the older brother, moved into the gigantic palace named Wilhelmsburg that had been built during his father's reign. He married, but his wife was unable to bear any children. His great disappointment at not having an heir motivated him to turn his energy towards the needs of Weimar and its people. Over time, Wilhelm Ernst improved the schools, began a vast library and antique coin collection, and introduced opera to his people.

His brother Johann Ernst III lived with his wife and children at the Red Palace, a much more modest building connected to Wilhelmsburg by a long red corridor. Although Johann Ernst died in 1707, shortly before Bach's arrival in Weimar, he was responsible for creating the court capelle and making music an important element in the lives of the Weimar people. It was this duke that Bach had worked for only five years ago.

Johann Ernst's son, Ernst-August, was not old enough to take his throne until 1709. For two years, Wilhelm Ernst ruled the land alone. When the time finally came for Ernst-August to assume his position, Wilhelm Ernst had a difficult time allowing his nephew, twenty-six years younger, to have any control over what he considered to be _his_ land.

Bach, always one to avoid political conflicts if at all possible, had no idea that he had left behind religious conflicts only to step into the middle of a political struggle between two dukes. He imagined a very exciting and dynamic life, playing a grand organ in the church built right into the Wilhelmsburg Palace, writing music, conducting the court capelle, and enjoying his highly respected title. He was the third-highest ranking musician employed by the court (just underneath the capellmeister and vice-capellmeister), a far cry from the "lackey" position he had held when he had been just a violinist in the court capelle.

Wilhelmsburg Palace at Weimar.

Having received a full month's salary up front, Bach moved his pregnant wife and himself into an upscale apartment in a house near the Market Square. Most of the employees of the court lived in this *Freyhaus* (free house), a boarding house five minutes' walking distance from Wilhelmsburg Palace. In December 1708, a few days after Catharina Dorothea was born, Maria Barbara's unmarried sister came to live with them. She would stay with the Bach family until her death in 1729, and she earned her room and board. She helped raise the children and keep the house clean.

The problem for Bach in his new job was that the two stubborn dukes were constantly arguing over who had control over the court musicians. Ernst-August of the Red Palace felt that they should be his servants, considering it was his father who had founded the orchestra in the first place. Duke Wilhelm Ernst, on the other hand, believed that since he was the senior ruler, all court servants belonged under his command. One feud began when Wilhelm Ernst created a rule that no

Duke Wilhelm Ernst of the court of Weimar. *(Courtesy of Staatliche Kunstsammlunger, Weimar.)*

member of the orchestra could perform at the Red Palace without his permission, which of course Ernst-August thought was unreasonable because his palace paid half of their salaries. Bach, as the most famous of all their musicians, was soon to be thrust even deeper into the middle of their tug-of-war, which would prove very tiring.

Also tiring were the strict laws enforced by the religiously zealous Duke Wilhelm Ernst. Anyone breaking his moral codes would be heavily punished, fined, or even thrown out of town if the offenses were too frequent. He would often test his servants on the sermons given in the chapel, and at one point he instituted a city-wide lights out policy. After nine o'clock (eight in the winter), children and grownups alike, including Bach himself, were forbidden to do any work or have any fun. Bach considered it an absurd law, mostly because he had always worked best in the late-night hours when his time belonged to him alone. That said, it should be noted that at least half of Bach's most famous organ works were written during his nine years in Weimar. It is easy to assume, given Bach's history of moonlight escapades, that he somehow found a way to work after hours without getting caught.

One of the projects Bach worked on during his free time in Weimar was something known as the "Little Organ Book." He bound together a book of blank pages and methodically filled them with 164 organ chorales written to make the songs in the Lutheran hymnbook sound more beautiful to his ear. Mostly he focused on the hymns he had known when he was a child, for there are no hymns in the "Little Organ Book" written after the year 1675. Originally he wrote it as a guide for church organists to use in their services, but ultimately he used the book as a teaching tool for his sons and many of his students. While in Weimar he had twelve pupils who came to him for private organ or harpsichord lessons, two having followed him all the way from Mühlhausen.

In 1711, Bach's predecessor to his role as court organist, Effler, died. It was at this time that Bach made his first political move. This was an era in which musicians, no matter how important or famous, were considered subservient to their noble masters. But Sebastian Bach was never afraid to ask for what he wanted. He submitted a request to Duke Wilhelm Ernst asking for the money Effler had received as a retirement salary. The Duke reluctantly agreed, and Bach got his first raise.

Bach now earned the same salary as the vice-capellmeister. Two years later he would get another raise to two hundred guilders a year, the same salary as the head capellmeister, who never had a raise in the entire thirty-three years that he served the palace. Despite the raises, the duke never promoted Bach in rank. It was his small way of keeping power over his strong-willed—and increasingly expensive—employee.

Bach asked the duke for more money in the summer of 1712. He wanted to do an expensive overhaul of the organ in the Wilhelmsburg chapel. The duke agreed, perhaps because he knew that Bach would want to oversee the work and would have little time to visit the Red Palace. From June 29 until December 23, 1712, the organ was dismantled. Bach and the carpenters worked day and night to get the wind box and bellows chambers ready in time for Christmas Eve services. It was a hectic time, and though the instrument was greatly improved, Bach knew it would never measure up to his standards. Although Bach was most famous in his lifetime for his expertise at the organ, sadly, he was never hired to play a first-class instrument on a permanent basis.

The lovely and ornate chapel at Wilhelmsburg palace.

Over at the Red Palace, Ernst-August had a twelve-year-old half brother, Prince Johann Ernst, who studied music. The young prince made a trip to Amsterdam, the publishing capital of the world, and returned with a huge collection of the newest published manuscripts. Among them was *L'Estro Armonico*, a set of concertos by the Italian composer Antonio Vivaldi. Bach was mesmerized by the music—it set a new standard for the way a concerto was written, with a fast-slow-fast movement structure that pitted the soloist against the orchestra in an exciting musical duel. Vivaldi's concertos were written for a violin soloist and orchestra, and Bach tried his hand at rearranging them for harpsichord and organ—mostly so he could perform them himself.

Italian Baroque music was much different than the music Bach was used to hearing. For one thing, the Italians were mostly Catholic, and they had different rules about how music was used in their daily church-going lives. The Catholics liked grandiose spectacles in their cathedrals and for their services. The more voices and instruments, the better—they even allowed women to sing and play instruments, which was very rare at the time. The North Germans, on the other hand, were mostly Protestant, and their religion took a more humble ap-proach to how music should be used in church. Though music was an important element in church services, it followed strict rules, with a limited use of ornamentation so that it would not distract from the purpose of worship.

In Italy, composers such as Arcangelo Corelli

Title page of Antonio Vivaldi's *L'Estro Armonico.*
*(Courtesy of British Library.)*

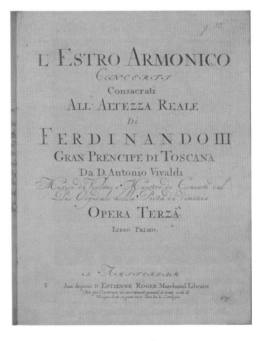

Italian composer and violinist Arcangelo Corelli.

and Tomaso Albinoni favored the violin in their lengthy concertos. In Germany, the *clavier* instruments (the harpsichord and organ) were preferred. Italian music reflected the sunny, mild climate in the south. German music was always a bit more somber, as though the colder weather blew through every measure.

The most important difference between the Italians and Germans, however, is that the Italians had a great love for music as entertainment. They had gala opera productions (theatrical plays that were sung from beginning to end), and built grand concert halls for performances. The Protestants did not believe in wasting their time with entertainment. The only chance the German people had to enjoy music was at church functions or, if they were so fortunate, in the courts of the princes and dukes who ruled the land.

Bach's discovery of Vivaldi was a watershed moment in his musical career. Hearing, playing, and studying Vivaldi's innovative music allowed Bach to rethink the way his compositions were put together. In the work that comes after his study of Vivaldi, Bach's musical signature takes on a new depth and richness. He was no longer merely a student of other composers. He now became a true master in his own right. His blending of Italian buoyancy into German complexity created an entirely

Antonio Vivaldi. *(Engraving by Lambert the Younger.)*

new kind of music and set the stage for the synthesis of different styles that influenced later musicians such as Wolfgang Amadeus Mozart.

Throughout his time in Weimar, Bach frequently received invitations from other cities and towns to come evaluate their organs or play dedication ceremonies. When Bach tested an organ he pushed the instrument's limits, testing the strength and capacity of the instrument's lungs. To do this he would literally pull out all the stops, blasting the organ for the loudest sound it could muster. The enormous sound would rattle the teeth of whoever had employed him, and Bach surely had more than one good laugh at the startled expressions on a church director's face.

In February of 1713, Bach was invited to the court of Saxe-Weissenfels for Duke Christian's twenty-first birthday. The event was held at a hunting lodge, so Bach was asked to compose a piece to celebrate the hunt. What Bach put together was an intricate cantata titled "Jubilant Dispute of the Gods," his first secular cantata (now referred to as the "Hunt Cantata"). Both of the Weimar dukes were in attendance, and the impressive performance by Bach made them proud. Bach made an excellent impression on Duke Christian as well, and he would eventually hire Bach as a composer for his own court capelle.

It was also in 1713 that Bach made a trip to the city of Halle to test the organ in Our Lady's Church. This massive instrument had sixty-five stops, and it must have excited Bach greatly when he saw it. What a joy it would be to have the post as organist in this church. The job was offered to him, and twenty-eight-year-old Bach had to decide if he should quit his cozy job at Weimar just to be able to play this wonderful instrument full-time. Ultimately, he had to think of his growing family— he now had three children to support along with his wife and sister-in-law. The salary Halle offered did not compare to what he was earning in Weimar, and he let them know it when turning down the offer. "It is not to be assumed that one will go to a place where one's situation is worsened," Bach wrote to the Halle Church Board.

Upon Bach's return to Weimar, he went straight to Duke Wilhelm Ernst and requested a promotion. The duke did grant Bach the new, more important title of concertmaster and a substantial raise in salary, probably out of gratitude that his prized musician had not abandoned him and also as a bribe to keep him from thinking of leaving in the future. To Bach's frustration, however, the new title, with its duties of performing one new church composition each month, was still the third-ranking position in the musician hierarchy. He was reaching a level of talent and fame that he felt deserved more respect.

What struck many about Bach's music was how effortless it seemed for him to write. Bach's complex counterpoint is so dense with levels of weaving melodies that it is like a mathematical puzzle. Bach had the ability to set out for himself the most difficult contrapuntal idea and to jot it down quickly between rehearsals. This music was not at all easy to play, even by later standards. The nineteenth century composer Felix Mendelssohn, most famous today as the composer of the *Wedding Recessional*, was one of the world's leading organists, and even he, who could play any piece of music at first sight, spent countless hours practicing Bach. But Bach could play his own compositions without so much as batting an eye. "His organ and clavier compositions," wrote a friend thirty-four years after the master's death, "are held to be difficult by everyone who knows them. But for him they were not so in the slightest; rather, he executed them with ease and skill."

For the next two years Bach enjoyed a quiet domestic life with his growing family, while at the same time composing music. Twice Bach composed massive works for important events at the Red Palace. One was for the funeral of Ernst-August's younger brother, and the other was for Ernst-August's wedding.

In December of 1716, the head capellmeister, Drese, died. Hoping that he would be promoted at last, Bach set to work right away, filling in as temporary music director until the duke made up his mind as to who would officially take over. Perhaps Bach thought that by writing three new cantatas three weeks in a row right before Christmas, he was making his case to inherit the job. He was, however, quite wrong to make this assumption.

The duke offered the job to Georg Philipp Telemann, Bach's good friend and the music director at Frankfurt. Telemann declined the offer by saying that the court already had the best musician in the land. Unmoved by Telemann's remark, the duke promoted Drese's son. Musicians of the era had very little political leverage and, although Bach wanted the job, the duke had political reasons to give it to someone else.

So there Bach was, second in rank to a musician far from his equal, writing some of the most innovative music in the country, and out of favor with his duke. It was time, yet again, to move on. Bach began to treat his invitations to other cities for organ performances as auditions; he kept his eyes open for opportunities to find better employment. Duke Ernst-August, of the Red Palace, must have felt a certain amount of sympathy for what was happening to Bach, so he arranged for Prince Leopold of Anhalt-Cöthen to consider hiring Bach as capellmeister of his court. The prince had heard Bach play at Ernst-August's wedding (the duke had married the prince's sister), so he was well acquainted with the organist's talent.

Early in 1717, Cöthen offered Bach a job. He was delighted to accept. Shortly thereafter, he was invited to play a concert in Dresden, the capital city of Saxony. Bach went, flush with the triumph of his new position. Dresden was a wonderful place to celebrate—

Duke Ernst August of Saxe-Weimar. *(Engraving by Johann Christoph Sysang, courtesy of Bach Archiv, Leipzig.).)*

like Venice in Italy and Versailles in France, Dresden was a vibrant and progressive court where the arts were much respected and admired. Bach arrived in Dresden to great acclaim. Here his skills were known and people clamored to hear him play.

The Dresden court employed an arrogant organist called Marchand le Grand (French for "the Great") who had previously worked for the royal court in France and had a reputation that rivaled Bach's. French music was considered more beautiful than German music, so Bach's fans conceived of a plan to pit organist against organist in a competition that would determine not just which man, but also which music, was supreme.

Bach was prevailed upon to write a letter to Marchand inviting him to play. He proposed each would have a chance to play and then the other would have to imitate that effort as best he could. The audience would determine the victor. Marchand agreed to the contest and the stage was set.

A large crowd gathered at Flemming Palace on the appointed night. Bach and his supporters arrived with much fanfare. The crowd was jolly and the mood festive. But as time passed, people became restless. Finally, a man was dispatched to Marchand's hotel to summon the Frenchman to the event. That messenger returned with the news that Marchand was gone: he had fled, by coach, in the middle of the night.

The audience roared at the news. Bach was implored to play alone, and he did. His concert was an enormous success and did much to boost his fame. He returned to Weimar in triumph, ready to pack up his belongings and move on.

Unfortunately for Bach, it was not that simple. The patronage system meant Bach could only leave if his employer let him. Rather than offering their wares for sale, musicians and other artists relied on patrons to support them. Usually members of the nobility, patrons offered food, lodging, and generally some recompense to the artists they favored. The artist was treated like any other member of the patron's staff, which meant the artist had little freedom and few rights. Bach had been treated well during his time at Weimar, but he did not show enough humility to Duke Wilhelm when he asked to be released. To show Bach his place, the duke had him put in jail.

Bach was not, however, put in the dungeons with the true criminals. On November 17, 1717 he was detained in the "County Judge's place of detention." For almost a month, he stayed under lock and key, unable to see his family or go about freely. Aside from the wound to his pride, the month of confinement was not a terrible ordeal. He was given paper and used the solitude to focus on composing. By the end of his sentence, Bach had begun a work for keyboard titled *The Well-tempered Clavier* and had filled the pages of the "Little Organ Book."

On December 2, Bach was "freed from arrest with notice of his unfavorable discharge." No more is known about why Bach was released from jail or even why he was put there in the first place. Salaries and expenses in this court were carefully recorded, but while the town ledger tells how much was spent on oats for the horses, it seldom mentions Johann Sebastian Bach. Even a book chronicling the great organ of Weimar, published in 1737, makes no reference to Bach.

One hundred years later, talented musicians would be able to demand the same respect accorded to the nobility, but to the court of Weimar, Sebastian Bach was no more than another tradesman passing through.

# Chapter Six
## A Time of Friendship and Love

The seven members of the Bach household left Weimar as quickly as possible once Bach was released from his imprisonment. They traveled seventy miles northeast to their new home and settled in the large apartment provided for them in a beautiful boarding house. It stood a few steps from the palace gate and had a rehearsal room downstairs. They unpacked just before Christmas, with little time to prepare for Bach's first big event in Cöthen, the annual New Year's celebration.

Cöthen was by far the smallest town in which Bach had been employed. It was part of the Anhalt region between the Harz Mountains and the River Elbe. At least thirty miles from the nearest city, Cöthen was quite isolated and very dull. What little news or gossip the citizens heard was from the messengers and trades

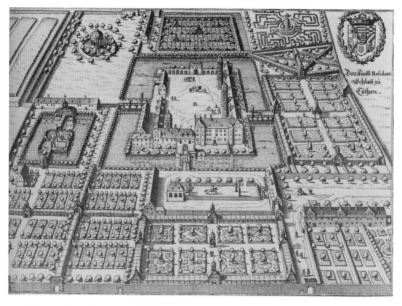

The castle and park in Cöthen. *(Courtesy of Archiv für Kunst und Geschichte.)*

people who passed through on their way from Hamburg to Leipzig.

There was little audience for entertainment in Cöthen. The central religion was Calvinism, a puritanical Protestant creed brought over from England that shunned worldly pleasures of any kind. There was one Lutheran church for the Bach family to attend, complete with a school for Bach's sons. This church did not have much of an organ, so Bach's skills in that area were not needed during his time in Cöthen. He used the organ for teaching purposes only. Nor did he focus on writing music for church services because little music was used.

The ruler of Cöthen, Prince Leopold, inherited his title at the age of ten and was only twenty-three when Bach came into his service. Leopold was raised as a

Calvinist and went loyally to his stark services every Sunday. But the other six days of the week, his palace was filled with music. The prince had done a tour of all the cultural centers of Europe four years earlier and was familiar with the latest styles in clothing, décor, art and music. His luxurious palace, which had been built in stages between 1587 and 1640, was most famous for its extensive gardens. The prince was famous for his love of all things beautiful.

Without any need to focus on the organ or church, Bach had more freedom in his compositions. It was during this time he wrote some of his most memorable works. Prince Leopold turned out to be a generous and pleasant leader, quite the opposite of the stingy court at Weimar. Money was waiting for Bach when he arrived because Leopold felt that Bach should be paid from the time he signed his contract of employment in August. Bach was thus paid for five months of work he did not do, which helped to make up for the month of imprisonment without pay in Weimar.

Also different from the Weimar dukes was Prince Leopold's attitude toward his musicians. He himself was an accomplished amateur musician, who enjoyed playing violin or harpsichord with the eighteen-member capelle. Because it was such a small town, the members of the orchestra spent a great deal of time together and became friends. Bach would remain close with many of these players throughout his life.

Leopold was very much a part of this circle; there was

little sense of distinction in rank. In Bach, the prince had found not only a musician of genuine merit, but a kindred spirit. Even though Bach was now thirty-two, nine years older than the prince, married and the father of several children, they had much in common. A testament to their friendship was that Prince Leopold became godfather to Sebastian and Maria Barbara Bach's seventh child, who was born November 15, 1718.

Prince Leopold of Anhalt-Cöthen. *(Engraving by Martin Bernigeroth.)*

The years Bach spent at Cöthen were, in many ways, the happiest of his life. Bach had a new friend in the prince, and he was finally getting the respect he deserved. For the first two and a half years of his employment there, Bach must have enjoyed his growing family and well-paid position. The good times were cut short, however, as one terrible event followed another in rapid succession, beginning with the death of his baby in 1719. The following summer, events took a turn for the worse.

Whenever Prince Leopold traveled he liked to take Bach and six or seven other members of the court capelle

with him. This way he could show off his talented collection of players to the other aristocrats. The fateful
summer of 1720, Prince Leopold had taken the entou-
rage to Carlsbad, a spa town where nobles from all over
Europe mingled. They stayed nearly three months, soak-
ing up the bubbly water and playing music.

News traveled so slowly that Bach did not find out
until he arrived home on his doorstep that Maria Barbara, his beloved wife of thirteen years, had taken seriously ill during his absence and died. He had not even
been able to attend her funeral, as she had been buried
three weeks before he returned home.

This was a time of deep grief for the musician. Co-
incidentally, it was during this same time that his
Brandenburg Concertos were finished. These six concertos, written for varying instruments and exemplify-
ing Italian and French Baroque music, are among the
most buoyant and well-known of Bach's works. They
also represent the advances he made in the concerto
genre: working from the French and Italian models he
studied, Bach added his own vision to create music that
was richer, more complex, livelier, and more dazzling.
They were also the last of his playful pieces. The
Brandenburg Concertos were presented to the youngest
son of the Prussian King, Margrave Christian Ludwig.
Today, they are some of the most often performed and
recorded musical works in the world.

His wife's death gave Bach time to think. His job at
Cöthen offered him comfort and creativity, but he was

doing little to glorify God. He began to look for a job that would put him at the keyboard of a church organ again.

After two months of grieving with his children, Bach took a trip to Hamburg. He had been invited to audition for the open post of organist at St. Jakob's Church. He would have liked to try for the job, but the auditions were planned for the week of Prince Leopold's birthday in early December. There was always a concert during the birthday celebrations, and Bach would not be able to get away. Bach did not want to pass on the job in Hamburg just because of a scheduling problem, so he went on his own, a month early, hoping he would get a chance to play the organ and impress the town council. Instead of slogging the long journey on foot as he had when a teenager, Bach traveled by mail coach, which was first-class travel in a fine covered vehicle.

In Hamburg, Bach was permitted to play the magnificent St. Catherine's organ that he had admired as a youth. Listening in the pews that evening was Reinken, Bach's idol, now almost one hundred years old. In his honor, Bach played the very same piece he had first heard the master play so many years ago. Of course, true to Bach's style, it was quite embellished. Reinken was impressed, urging him to play for another two hours, most of which he spent improvising preludes. Later, Reinken wrote to Bach of his skill at the organ: "I thought this art was dead, but I see that it still lives in you."

Bach was offered the job at Hamburg, and probably

Bach traveled to Hamburg after his wife's death. *(Courtesy of Deutsche Staatsbibliothek, Berlin.)*

would have accepted if not for the Hamburg town council's announced desire to accept the gift of a donation from whomever they hired. It was common practice at the time to offer positions for sale, and the Hamburg council had considered auctioning off the organist's job, eventually deciding that it was a religious position and the practice might look unseemly.

After Bach turned them down, the people of Hamburg selected a new organist, a man of no real acclaim named J. Joachim Heitmann. Upon accepting his post, Heitmann donated four thousand marks to the Hamburg town council.

Johann Matheson, Cantor of Hamburg's cathedral, railed against the town council:

> If such conditions are to prevail in our city, then the next time there is a competition for organist and one of the angels from Bethlehem decides to come down from Heaven and desires to be organist of St. Jakob's church and plays divinely but has no money to offer, there will be nothing for him to do but to fly away again.

The position at Hamburg would have been ideal. Bach

was frustrated to miss out on his chance to play on such a marvelous organ. But his family did not have the money Heitmann did, nor would Bach's pride have allowed him to buy a position he had easily earned. Returning to Cöthen, Bach devoted himself to his family.

Bach was now the sole head of the household. Maria Barbara had carried out this duty with extraordinary organization and patience, but it was too much for his sister-in-law to do alone. Every day he was reminded there were four children depending on him for food and attention. Meals, which were cooked on an open flame, took hours to prepare, and there was no refrigeration, so food tended to spoil if not planned well and used quickly. Bach did not have time to take care of daily chores. He had concerts to play, choruses to conduct, and music to compose. Despite all of his responsibilities, being a dedicated father to his children was more important to him than fame and fortune. In fact, from this point on he would make many career decisions by putting the needs of his family before his own personal ambition.

In this era a widower could not stay single for long. A wife was necessary. Bach took an unusually long time, a year and a half, before he remarried. He did not want to marry the first woman that came along, as his father had. The woman Bach married would need to take good care of her stepchildren and be quite exceptional to replace his beautiful and dearly missed first love. Luckily, Bach found that woman in Anna Magdalena Wülcken.

They met when he and Prince Leopold were hiring

female voices to sing the birthday and New Year's cantatas Bach had written. This twenty-year-old beauty was the daughter of a trumpet player from a nearby town. She had a wonderful singing voice. Over time Bach put his grief for his first wife aside and fell deeply in love with Anna Magdalena.

Anna Magdalena seemed hardly the best match for Bach. She was a young, inexperienced girl who was, by all accounts, headstrong. The doubters would be proven wrong. Anna and Sebastian remained happily married for the rest of Bach's life—twenty-eight years. They would have thirteen children together, although only six would survive childhood. Anna was a great friend and support to her husband. She took on the job of copying his compositions for him and their handwriting became almost identical. Today it is difficult for people studying Bach's manuscripts to detect which are in Anna's hand and which are in Bach's. He dedicated many pieces to her, most notably a small notebook of works for the clavier called the *Anna Magdalena Notebook*. Even after the marriage, Bach encouraged Anna to continue singing in the Cöthen court capelle. They were a working couple, which may be common today but was quite rare in the eighteenth century.

One week after Bach's wedding, Prince Leopold married Frederica Henrietta of Anhalt-Bernburg. She was a petite vision with porcelain skin, like a living doll. The new princess demanded all of Prince Leopold's time and had no interest in music. Bach even took to calling her *amusa*, or enemy of the muses. Leopold's close friendship with Bach began to suffer because, in an effort to please his beautiful new music-indifferent wife, he no longer asked for new music to be written for the palace.

Bach's output from the time reflects his patron's indifference. He went from composing large public pieces like the Brandenburg Concertos and *Orchestral Suites,* to refocusing on keyboard music. One of these works, *The Well-tempered Clavier,* would turn out to be among his most important pieces. Today piano students use the forty-eight preludes and fugues in this set as a test of excellence—if one can play all of these pieces, one can play anything. But it was actually written as Bach's declaration of the importance of the system of tuning he had helped bring to prominence, something called equal temperament.

To tune an instrument means to measure the distance between notes so that the pitches are equal. When we

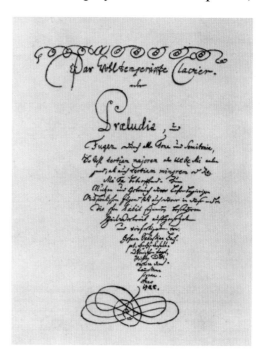

Title page of *The Well-tempered Clavier* (1722).
*(Courtesy of Deutsche Staatsbibliothek, Berlin.)*

play a piano today, we expect a C to sound like a C no matter which C we hit on the keyboard or which piano we play. This is called well-tempered, or equal-tempered, tuning. Before Bach's time this style of tuning was not widely used. The way that strings vibrate against each other naturally puts some in tune and some out of tune. Players of keyboard instruments would tune the strings to the key of the music they were going to play, with only the notes that they required having the correct pitch. Any unneeded strings would be left out of tune. The biggest problem with this method of tuning was that if an organist or harpsichord player wanted to play a second piece in a different key, he would have to stop the recital and retune the strings before he could go on with his performance.

The Baroque era was a time of great musical innovation. Instruments were being both invented and refined, and musical compositions grew more complex. Several scholars gave their attention to devising a better system of tuning keyboard instruments and the results, while still imperfect, allowed musicians to modulate the key of a piece without having to stop to retune their instruments.

Bach was quite taken by the idea of equal temperament and composed a number of works to be played in multiple keys, most notably the *Chromatic Fantasy and Fugue*, which used many keys and could only be played on a tempered instrument. Bach also used *The Well-tempered Clavier* to demonstrate the effectiveness of this tuning process by writing two sets of preludes and fugues in every key. He finished the first set in 1722 and the second set twenty years later. Composers today regard these two volumes of preludes and fugues as an invaluable tool of study, but they were never published during Bach's lifetime.

Portrait of Johann Sebastian Bach, c. 1720. *(Courtesy of Bachhaus, Eisenach.)*

Evidently, the free time to work on his personal projects had its benefits. At the age of thirty-seven, though, Bach was being forced into retirement, and this did not please the composer at all. He still wanted to perform and have his works played in public. It was, yet again, time he found another job.

In 1723, a messenger came with the news that a position had become available when Johann Kuhnau, the St. Thomas School Choirmaster in Leipzig, died. The messenger did not have a job offer in his hands, but he did invite Bach to come to Leipzig to apply. Bach was anxious to accept this post, since Leipzig was almost as important and cosmopolitan a city as Hamburg. After a year of total idleness (and probably restlessness for Bach, who was used to working very hard all the time), he considered the message from Leipzig very seriously. He had never enjoyed teaching in the classroom before, but this setting would be more like St. Matthew's in Lüneburg, with serious-minded students and a prestigious job title.

For his audition, Bach would play the Good Friday service on March 26, 1723. He wrote a magnificent work called *St. John Passion*. A Passion is a cantata, a choral retelling of the life and death of Jesus Christ. In this case, the story of the crucifixion is drawn from the book of John in the Bible's New Testament (which is why it is called *St. John Passion* and not St. John's Passion—it is the passion story according to John, not the story of John's own passion). After the performance, the town council unanimously elected Bach into the position of cantor at the prestigious St. Thomas School.

Prince Leopold had no problem releasing Bach from his position in the Cöthen court. He knew that it was not fair to keep Bach cooped up any longer and was pleased that his talents would be put to good use. Less than a year after Bach left Cöthen the princess died, but it was too late for Bach to change his situation and return. Prince Leopold became ill and died only five years later. Bach wrote a touching cantata to commemorate this noble lord who had shined brightly for too short a time.

# Chapter Seven
## Classes and Cantatas

When Bach and his family arrived in Leipzig on May 22, 1723, the local weekly newspaper had this to say: "Last Saturday at noon four wagons loaded with household goods arrived here from Cöthen; they belonged to the former Princely Music Director there, now called to Leipzig as Cantor Figuralis. He himself arrived with his family in two carriages, at two o'clock and moved into his newly renovated residence at the Thomas school." Leipzig town records of Bach's early years in the cantorship often referred to him by his Cöthen court title, their way of displaying that they had hired someone of value. After all, it was Bach's great reputation for the organ works, cantatas, and choral oratorios he had written at his former posts of Weimar and Cöthen that helped him to get this post. The former Cantor, a man named

Looking to the west above the city of Leipzig. *(Courtesy of Museum für Geschichte der Stadt, Leipzig.)*

Johann Kuhnau, had let some of his responsibilities slide in the last few years before he died, and Bach was expected to come in and shape things up. Little did the town council know that Bach would take his job so seriously that he would go far beyond what they expected or even desired of him.

Leipzig was one of the largest cities in the region of Saxony, boasting thirty thousand inhabitants. It hosted four main churches, the St. Thomas School, a town hall for civic meetings, a municipal library, and one of the most prestigious universities in all of Germany. The streets were cobblestone, many people lived in their own private houses, and just outside the wall enclosing the town were tailored gardens and tree-lined walkways. Between the moat and the River Pleisse were a number of coffeehouses, where the upper classes would come to socialize and hear music. The publishing and printing trades drew a lot of industry, and the beauty of the city brought many tourists. The town council hoped that Bach's music would draw tourists as well.

Bach's family of eight (with a newborn girl, Anna's first child) was to live in the St. Thomas school building. The top three floors of the four-story west wing were reserved for their personal space, and it was by far the largest living quarters the family had ever inhabited. They split three bedrooms on the fourth floor, played and ate on the third, and Bach's study and library were on the second floor. Bach particularly enjoyed his study because the window overlooked the gardens outside the town wall. By this point in his life, Bach had amassed quite a collection of rare, antique music, and the shelves of his study were lined with books and manuscripts. The school's library of music was also kept in the cantor's study, though many of these books were in poor shape, having been chewed by mice or worn by use and time. Still, the collection amounted to hundreds of books for Bach's ever-hungry eyes.

Bach was eager to get to work—there was much to be done. The duties of the St. Thomas cantor included writing and organizing music for four churches, teaching the choirs who would perform at the church services,

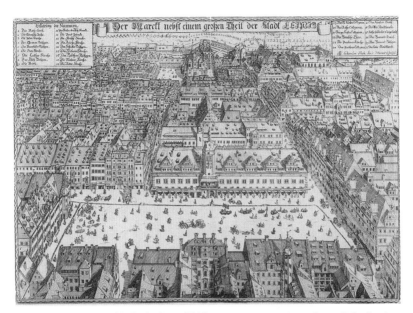

Panoramic view of Leipzig from 1712. *(Engraving by Johann Georg Schreiber.)*

giving instrumental lessons to students of the school, and teaching Latin classes. The city also had a town band of four wind players and four string players that Bach led, and he hoped to do work with the *collegium musicum*, a choir and instrumental group made up of young men from the university. Kuhnau had let the relationship between the cantor and collegium deteriorate, but Bach could not stand the thought of those wonderfully trained voices not being put to good use. For all this hard work, he only earned one-fourth of the salary he had received in Cöthen, which meant he had to pick up extra money performing at weddings and funerals.

Soon after arriving, Bach decided he would not use any of the existing textbooks and began to create all of his own teaching materials. He also threw out all the cantatas and chorales that the previous cantors had been using in the Sunday services. He did not think they were of high enough quality. He wrote a new cantata every week during the first five years of his employment at Leipzig. Though these pieces were only twenty minutes in length, it was no easy task. First he selected the text, and then he wrote the music to which the words would be set. He printed booklets of the cantatas for his singers and instrumentalists to use during performances. He paid for the printing out of pocket, but often earned his money back by selling copies to wealthy music lovers. A booklet usually held six cantatas, and he would create twelve booklets per year. Of the hundreds of booklets made, only five exist today.

Bach's first Leipzig cantata was preformed at the end of May. The university newspaper reported it was met "with good applause." The next day, the first of June, a small ceremony was held at St. Thomas School to welcome the new teacher. It was attended by the important members of the town and included a performance by the student choir. On this day Bach met the men who would attempt to control his work over the next twenty-seven years. These included penny-pinching town councilmen who cared more about cost and efficiency than they did about art, teachers who would rather have more science in the curriculum than music, and church directors who preferred simple and forgettable church programs. This event is hardly noteworthy except for one incident. Just after the chairman of the school board made a formal speech introducing Bach, the church pastor jumped up to make his own remarks on the occasion. The interruption of the ceremony offended the chairman deeply. He did not like any break from established protocol. After the ceremony, angry letters were fired off between the church and the city councils, whose offices were located three hundred feet from one another. The addition of a single sentence of welcome in a poorly attended ceremony had caused the dispute, and Bach no doubt wondered what he had gotten himself into.

If the chairman, one of the three burgomasters running the town, was offended by this small break in protocol, he had no idea how much his patience would be taxed in the years to come by Bach's ceaseless creativity. The town council knew Bach had a reputation for

The St. Thomas church and school, in the eighteenth century. *(Courtesy of Bach Archiv, Leipzig.)*

testing authority, so they had written into his contract that he was to introduce no innovations into the curriculum. Even though Bach signed this contract, he had no intention of obeying it. In fact, he was ready to make changes as soon as he heard the boys of St. Thomas School sing.

Fifty-four boys lived in the St. Thomas School dormitory. As Bach had done in his Lüneburg days, the boys attended school on scholarship. In exchange for their free education, they were required to sing in the various church choirs and at civic performances. Having listened to each boy sing, Bach remarked that "seventeen are competent, twenty not yet fully, and seventeen incapable." He had no choice but to use these boys, so he immediately formulated a plan to get the best out of them. He created four choirs. The very best singers would perform Bach's cantatas on alternate Sundays at the two largest churches of St. Thomas and St. Nicholas. The second choir sang only motets—choral works without an orchestra. This choir was not directed by Bach, but by a student, and alternated between the two large churches on opposite weeks from the first choir. A third choir, also student-led, sang motets and hymns at the smaller New Church. The fourth and weakest choir sang only hymns at the smallest church, St. Peter's. One might call Bach's reorganization of the choir innovations, but no one questioned his decisions.

At first, no one complained about his work as a teacher, either. Along with the boarding students, an-

The interior of St. Nicholas's Church. *(Courtesy of Evangelisch-lutherische, Leipzig.)*

other fifty or so sons of Leipzig families attended the school. These boys, ages thirteen through nineteen, were not well disciplined. Kuhnau had never been able to control them. However, there was never a single remark about discipline issues when Bach was leading the classes. Either the students feared the master, who had a sharp tongue and accepted nothing but excellent work, or they respected him for what he tried to accomplish. There were existing punishments for poor behavior, and Bach was asked to enforce them. Every fourth week it was his turn to serve as inspector in charge of making sure the boys got up at five A.M., dressed, and said their prayers before breakfast. There were monetary fines for mistakes in their lessons, and for messiness and mischievous behavior. The money would be taken out of the pay the students earned for their performances. Bach took this work very seriously, and the boys knew they had a hard taskmaster.

Although Bach enjoyed teaching, he only liked teaching music. He had no interest in spending twelve hours a week in non-musical classes. He solved the problem by hiring other teachers to take most of his Latin classes. The council knew about these arrangements and for a while they were content, especially after the tremendous work Bach did with the choirs that first Christmas season, when he methodically spread them out over the holiday to perform a variety of complicated works. One of those pieces was the Magnificat in E-flat major, one of Bach's most difficult choral pieces. A magnificat is a musical setting of the hymn the Virgin Mary sings in the Gospel of Luke when she realizes that she will be giving birth to the Savior. It was a Protestant tradition to have a magnificat performed on Christmas Eve, and Bach's version was a truly inspired work that the people of Leipzig greatly admired.

One would think Bach had enough on his plate to keep him satisfied, but he was not content. The university had its own church, St. Paul's, and in the past the cantor of St. Thomas was responsible for the services there. However, in the six months between Kuhnau's death and Bach's hiring, the university decided to give the job to a man named J. Gottlieb Görner. It was one of the steps the university had taken in order to separate itself from the Leipzig government. The university director neglected to tell the town council that he had made this decision, and the council told Bach that he would be in charge of the music at St. Paul's. Bach rightfully considered the job, and the extra income, to be his.

Bach petitioned the council many times, hoping that they would intervene on his behalf. Eventually, in 1725, after two long years, it was decided that Görner and Bach would split the two services between them and also split the salary. Furious, Bach took this matter straight to King Augustus I in Dresden. The King, undoubtedly having other more pressing matters on his mind, ruled that Bach would run half the services at the full fee, but that the university could assign the rest to whomever they liked. Bach accepted the deal and then decided he did not care to do the work after all. He delegated his duties to his apprentices.

By 1729 Bach's relationship with the town council had begun to sour. The forty-four year old cantor tested the limits of his contract whenever possible. He always wanted more control. When music positions became available, he nudged his own students and favorite colleagues into the jobs, so that all the musicians in town were among his allies and would do his bidding.

Then Bach pushed too far. For Easter 1729 Bach had written a new Passion. Thanks to his *St. John Passion* (which he had used for his audition in 1723 and played again on Easter 1724) this new work was greatly anticipated by the people of Leipzig. Bach had been working on this piece since 1708, and would continue to tinker with it for the rest of his life. This work, called *St. Matthew Passion*, is for huge forces, complete with two organs, two orchestras, two choruses, a harpsichord, and five solo singers. It lasts over three hours. Recounting the story of Jesus Christ's experiences from the Last Supper through his Resurrection from the perspective of Matthew,

Bach's manuscript for *St. John Passion,* which had been performed to great enthusiasm in Leipzig in 1725. *(Courtesy of Staatsbibliothek Preussischer Kulturbesitz, Berlin.)*

*St. Matthew Passion* is the largest-scale work that Bach ever wrote and speaks more about his devotion to his religion than any other piece of music he composed. This Passion mattered so much to him, in fact, that Bach scribbled prayers such as "Jesus, help me" in the margins of the score as he composed.

Bach had only three weeks to rehearse this extremely demanding music, which put him under a lot of pressure. These must have been fast and frantic rehearsals, the perfectionist composer pacing back and forth, pounding on the organ, and trying to be in many places at once. Bach once even threw his wig at Görner just for missing an entrance on the organ. Though he had the best musicians available at the time, they were still not quite up to the challenge of this thoroughly modern work.

In the end, Bach was not pleased with the performance. Today we can attend a concert or hear a recording of *St. Matthew Passion* sung with amazing precision, but in Bach's era choirs (particularly student ensembles) were simply not able to make sense of the dense counterpoint, let alone the musical drama. When the town clerk once asked Bach if he would compose another Passion, Bach's response must have been quite dour, for the clerk reported that Bach had told him "he did not care, for he got nothing out of it anyway… and it was only a burden." The *St. Matthew Passion* wouldn't be heard again for a hundred years.

The town council was not concerned about the glory of Bach's music; they were disappointed with his service. They met to discuss grievances about the unruly cantor at St. Thomas's School. In the recorded minutes of a meeting, one complaint after another was hurled. They were upset that Bach was shrugging off his classes onto inferior teachers. They did not like his music. One member of the board even remarked in exasperation, "The choirmaster does nothing!" The decision was made to cut Bach's salary and to keep a closer eye on the auditions for the school choir and orchestra.

A few months later, in October of 1730, Bach wrote to an old friend of his, Georg Erdmann. His old schoolmate had become a diplomat in Poland. This letter is the closest Bach ever came to writing an autobiography, and his words explain very well the situation up until that point:

> …at first, indeed, it did not seem at all proper to me to change my position of Capellmeister [in Cöthen] for that of Cantor [in Leipzig]. Wherefore, then, I postponed my decision for a quarter of a year; but this post was described to me in such favorable terms that finally (particularly since my sons seemed inclined toward university studies) I cast my lot, in the name of the Lord, and made the journey to Leipzig… Here, by God's will, I am still in service. But since 1) I find that the post is by no means as lucrative as it had been described to me; 2) I have failed to obtain many of the fees pertaining to the office; 3) the place is very expensive; and 4) the authorities are odd and little interested in music, so that I must live amid almost continual vexation, envy and persecution; accordingly I shall be forced, with God's help, to seek my fortune elsewhere. Should Your Honor know or find a suitable post in your city for an old and faithful servant, I beg you most humbly to put in a most gracious word of recommendation for me—and I shall not fail to do my best to give satisfaction and justify your most gracious intercession on my behalf.

This is the letter of an unhappy man, trapped in a city that does not appreciate his innovations and slaps restrictions on him out of a deeply rooted fear of change. Bach wanted out, but leaving was not an option. His passionate plea gained him nothing. Erdmann never even answered his letter. Bach was forced to stay in Leipzig where, after seven years composing some of the world's most beautiful music, the forty-five-year-old composer must have felt completely hopeless. History would prove that at this time Bach was at the height of his creative powers, but, for Bach, it was likely a period of sadness and even desperation.

# Chapter Eight
## The Final Years

Johann Sebastian Bach had never been one to put up with petty town councils or jobs that were restrictive and confining. By tolerating his treatment in Leipzig, Bach hardly seems the same man he was years earlier in Arnstadt, Mühlhausen, or Weimar. The time had come to think about more than his own selfish desires. He had a large, growing family, and wanted the best for his children. If getting his boys a sophisticated education meant he had to subsume his own ambition, then so be it.

When the family had arrived in Leipzig in 1723, Bach's oldest son Wilhelm Friedemann was twelve years old and Carl Philipp Emanuel was nine. Bach had immediately put them into studies at St. Thomas School. Now, in 1730, both boys were enrolled at the university, and Bach's third son J. Gottfried Bernhard was attending St.

Thomas. When the sons born to Anna Magdalena were old enough, they would go to school in Leipzig as well. The boys made Bach proud. He said of his family, "They are born musicians, and I can assure you that I can already form an instrumental assembly within my own family, particularly since my present wife, Anna Magdalena, sings a good, clear soprano, and my eldest daughter, too, joins in not badly." In the Bach household, the family would be up early every morning, usually singing hymns before Bach had to begin work for the day at seven A.M. If visitors were in town, the family would sing and play music in the hours after supper as well. Bach enjoyed sharing his musical knowledge with all the members of his family, and he proudly showed off whenever he could.

One of Bach's greatest joys was to invite noted visiting musicians to his home for dinner parties and private concerts. He liked to meet and converse with every musical peer he could, and to discuss music theories with them. Most composers and virtuosos of the era were happy to take time out of their schedules to meet the cantor of Leipzig, who was so well known for his organ works. But there was a certain musician that Bach never got to meet. George Frideric Handel and Sebastian Bach were almost exactly the same age and had grown up in towns less than fifty miles apart, but they never once stood face to face. Handel spent most of his adult life in England and Italy writing operas, but at least twice he had come back to visit his hometown of Halle, thirty miles from Leipzig. The first time, Bach hurried over to Halle, but Handel left just hours before Bach arrived. The second time, Bach was sick with a fever, so he sent an invitation for Handel to come to Leipzig. Handel apparently did not see any particular benefit to meeting a schoolteacher and organist—he was a renowned opera composer after all—and he declined the offer.

The years 1729 and 1730 were bleak ones for Bach, but they were not without high points. It was in March of 1729 that Bach was officially awarded the director-ship of the collegium musicum. He had often used the university musicians in many of his cantatas, but now he would be able to write works specifically for them. Bach had less desire to write church music. He had written about three hundred cantatas since arriving in Leipzig, and that was plenty to keep the congregation from getting bored. Bach now dedicated most of his composing efforts to the collegium musicum.

The choir and orchestra made weekly performances at a charming place known as Zimmerman's Café. The wealthier citizens of Leipzig made the various Leipzig coffeehouses their main places for entertainment. There they would smoke, drink coffee, and read periodicals to learn of the fashions and current events of the day. All the while the collegium would play out in the open air on the verandas in front of the building. It was a lovely setting.

Bach wrote some lively, even humorous, music for the collegium. A biographer who had known Bach wrote of him that, "notwithstanding the main tendency of his genius to the great and sublime, he sometimes composed and performed something gay and even jocose; his cheerfulness and joking were those of a sage." He wrote a number of satirical works, the most famous of which was called *Coffee Cantata*, a piece making good-natured fun of upper-class ladies addicted to coffee—some of whom were frequent patrons of Zimmerman's Café, and who enjoyed laughing at Bach's parody.

Writing for the collegium inspired Bach to focus on music for the harpsichord. It is during the decade he

A cantata rehearsal. Bach's cantatas were some of his most popular compositions.

spent with the collegium that Bach wrote a four-part series of clavier works called *Clavier-Übung* (keyboard exercises). These were sort of like musical textbooks for those who played harpsichord or organ, for they featured a variety of forms that could be played on those instruments. Categories represented in these vol-

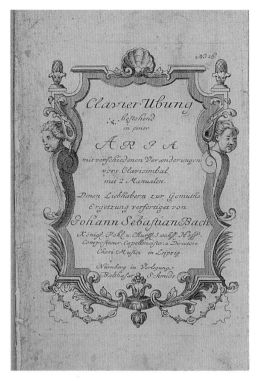

Title page of Bach's *Clavier-Übung. (Courtesy of British Library.)*

umes were suites, concertos, preludes, fugues and chorale settings. They represented the sounds of French, Italian and German music, all done Bach's way. Despite its uninspired name, the music was really quite extraordinary, and the four sections eventually earned their own nicknames such as the *French Suites* and *Italian Concertos*. Bach published these works with his own money and hired four young men to sell them in different towns. He also spent much of the 1730s writing the second set of *The Well-tempered Clavier*.

In 1730, Bach was given some hope of better work

environs when a new headmaster came to the St. Thomas School. The new man was J. Matthias Gesner, a friend of Bach's from Weimar. Whereas Bach's agreement stipulated no innovations, Gesner must have struck an entirely different deal with the council, for right after he arrived he began a thorough overhaul of the school's curriculum. He abandoned a Latin textbook written in 1595 for a text with a more modern approach. He also instituted a study of classical authors, and created more rigorous courses in higher math, geography, and natural history. He even added courses in art and physical education, an unheard of practice in those days.

One of the most important things Gesner did was to arrange for the renovation of the school building itself. Nearly two hundred years old, it was in terrible disrepair. The windows were drafty and the floors filthy. Many of the Leipzig aristocrats had begun refusing to send their children to the school. The repairs lasted from May of 1730 to June of 1732.

Gesner proved Bach's champion in other ways as well. The new headmaster finally freed the composer of his obligation to teach Latin classes, and, in a rather astonishing move, Gesner created a new hierarchy in the school so that Bach would only have to answer to the headmaster, not the frustrating town council. Gesner also restored Bach's full salary and saw to it that he was granted generous leaves of absence.

Bach made two journeys to Dresden in 1733. Once he went to help his son Wilhelm Friedemann get a job as

The city of Dresden, as painted by Bernardo Bellotto in 1748. (Courtesy of Gemäldegalerie, Dresden.)

organist at St. Sophie's Church, and on the second trip he applied for a job as court composer in Dresden. He had continued composing from abroad for the Cöthen court until Prince Leopold died, and now was occasionally composing pieces for Prince Christian in Saxe-Wessenfels. Bach thought he could do the same for King Augustus II of Poland. He sent the king two sections of his latest work.

King Augustus did not respond to Bach's submission, so Bach wrote to Count von Keyserlingk, a member of the Dresden court who was a great fan of his work. Keyserlingk vouched for the aging composer, and Augustus at last, three long years after Bach's initial application, decided to hire him. In gratitude, Bach performed a two-hour recital on the new organ at St. Sophie's Church for the king and his court.

It was during this happy time that Bach wrote his

*Christmas Oratorio*, which is one of the most cheerful and uplifting works he composed—quite a contrast to the long, pensive, agitated *St. Matthew Passion*. It was performed in Leipzig on six separate nights (one section per evening) between Christmas of 1734 and January of 1735, as a series of cantatas that form the larger whole.

The *Christmas Oratorio* provides an example of how Bach sometimes reused parts of older works in new pieces. Today we call this practice parody. Composers who had very little time to write important works for a funeral or other unexpected occasions often used parody to help them write quickly. The death of an important person, for example, called for a musical tribute equal to that person's status in life, but one or two days was often all the time available. A composer might use a previously written work, making some changes as time and necessity dictated. Bach's *St. Matthew Passion* is

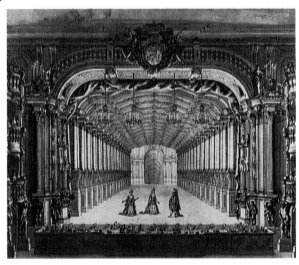

Inside the Dresden opera house. Bach traveled to the city several times with his son, Wilhelm Friedemann, in order to attend the opera there. *(Courtesy of Kupferstichkabinett, Dresden.)*

another of his works that revisits old themes.

The good years in Leipzig came to an end when Gesner was offered a better post in Göttingen in 1734. The Leipzig town council was not happy with the changes Gesner had brought to their school. A young man named J. August Ernesti replaced Gesner. Twenty years younger than Bach, Ernesti had some new ideas about what the students at St. Thomas should be learning. He felt that their studies should reflect what the boys would need to know in order to have good careers. For the first two years, Bach and Ernesti got along well enough. Ernesti was even chosen to be godfather to two of Bach's children. But things changed when Ernesti began to display his negative opinions toward the study of music, and before long the two men quit getting along at all.

In a private school setting, a prefect is a top student in the highest class chosen by a teacher to help monitor the other students. Bach made good use of prefects at St. Thomas; four of them helped direct the various choirs because Bach could not be everywhere at once. For one wedding in 1736, Bach asked one of his prefects, a boy named Gottfried Theodor Krause, to keep the younger choirboys in line during the services. The boys misbehaved so much up in the choir loft that they disrupted the wedding, and Krause was very embarrassed. He punished them by whacking them with a cane—too severe a response to their behavior. Headmaster Ernesti learned of the discipline and ordered that Krause be whipped by a cane in public in return for his lack of judgment. Not only was Ernesti's interference a serious undermining of Bach's authority, it would be a devastating blow to Krause's pride. Krause ran away.

With Krause gone, Ernesti quickly took another liberty. He appointed a new prefect, a student Bach considered a buffoon. Bach was furious about the appointment. Twice, upon entering the choir loft during Sunday services and seeing the new prefect there, Bach chased him out, shouting. From this point on, Ernesti and Bach would battle over every prefect appointment, as well as everything else they could think of. As a report of the time admits, "The situation between him and Ernesti developed to the point of charge and countercharge, and the two men from that time on were enemies."

Bach began to occupy himself less with the school. He chose to focus mainly on his family and music for the collegium. His sons were certainly keeping him busy throughout the 1730s. In 1734, Carl Philipp Emanuel graduated from the university and left to study law in Frankfurt. A year later Bach's third son, J. Gottfried Bernhard, graduated from St. Thomas School and applied for a job as organist in Mühlhausen. Bach helped all his sons get started in their careers by using his vast connections, writing letters of reference, or helping them with their audition material. For Gottfried, he had to do even more.

Gottfried could not control his spending and consistently got himself in trouble with creditors. Shortly after starting work in Mühlhausen, he got himself into terrible debt. Bach stepped in and wrote to Sangerhausen, asking them for some assistance. This was the town where, in 1702, the young Sebastian Bach had been offered a job only to have the duke intervene and appoint his own man to the position. The town council had been deeply upset about Bach's rebuff and was happy to right that past wrong by hiring Gottfried. No sooner had Gottfried assumed his new post than he was in trouble again. This time, in the spring of 1738, he fled, leaving no word of where he was going. In desperation, Bach wrote to a friend, "What shall I say or do further? Since no admonition or even any loving care and assistance will suffice any more, I must bear my cross in patience and leave my unruly son to God's Mercy alone..." The story ends tragically, for Gottfried died that May of fever, only twenty-four years old. Bach mourned deeply over his son's death.

As the 1740s approached, fifty-four year old Bach must have felt defeated. He would have happily retired from his job as cantor, but men did not retire in that era— they worked until they died. Bach simply began to slow down. He would rarely write any new music for the school or the churches, only reworking old pieces, and he gave up the collegium in 1741. He wrote fewer commissioned works and performed less frequently in public. If he gave concerts, they were usually in his own home for guests at dinner parties.

In 1742, Bach finished his fourth and final volume of the *Clavier-Übung*. History would come to know this last installment of harpsichord arrangements as the *Goldberg Variations*. A delightful story is told about how this music got its unofficial title. One of Bach's former students, J. Theophilus Goldberg, turned out to be a virtuoso at the harpsichord. At the age of fifteen he was hired to be Count von Keyserlingk's personal musician in Dresden. The count suffered from terrible insomnia and wanted the boy to play light music for him throughout the long nights. Goldberg wrote to his former teacher, asking if Bach had anything that he could use to fill these waking hours. Bach thought that his fourth edition of *Clavier-Übung* would do the trick. Keyserlingk, always a great admirer of Bach's work, adored these pieces and reportedly would wake in the middle of the night and ask his young harpsichordist, who slept in the room next to his, "Dear Goldberg, do play me my variations."

Although the work was not originally written for Keyserlingk (and was printed before Bach could dedicate it to this patron), the count was very grateful for the wonderful music and repaid Bach's efforts by giving him a golden goblet. It was the most generous gift anyone had ever given Bach.

In 1747, Bach took his famous trip to Berlin to see his son Carl Philipp Emanuel, harpsichordist in the court capelle of Frederick II, king of Prussia. It was on this trip to the Prussian court that Frederick surprised Bach with an invitation to try his hand at the pianoforte—playing Frederick's own music. The six-part fugue he improvised that night eventually became *The Musical Offer-*

*ing.* He sent the work to the king with many complimentary words. No money was ever sent to Bach, so we know that this offering was intended to be a gift to his son's employer. We can only assume that the king enjoyed his present, for there is no record of any reply of gratitude for the work.

Bach spent the rest of the 1740s laboring at two of his most important works. His *B-minor Mass* took thirty-five years to complete and was never performed in its entirety during his lifetime. This piece was not commissioned for a specific event or by a specific person. Bach wrote it only for the pleasure it brought him. The *B-minor Mass* shows Bach's transcendence of conventional form at its best. In it he challenges assumptions about the fundamental nature of sacred music by mixing prayers with songs and dances and stately fugues with lively concertos. Today the *B-minor Mass* is widely recognized to be one of the most important pieces of religious music ever composed.

The counterpart to the *B-minor Mass* is *The Art of*

Bach spent much of his life working on this piece of music, the *B-minor mass.* *(Courtesy of Staatsbibliothek Preussischer Kulturbesitz, Berlin.)*

*Fugue.* If his Mass took choral music to new heights, *The Art of Fugue* represents the pinnacle of fugal technique. This piece is not written for any specific instruments. Rather, it is a catalog of techniques for fugue writing that is still studied today by composition students. This was the piece Bach most wanted published—he pursued having the huge copper plates engraved for the printer, so undoubtedly it was a work of which he was very proud. Today it is considered the last of the great fugal compositions, for the new generation of composers preferred a lighter sound to their music—tunes with light accompaniment, ditties, as Sebastian would sometimes call them. Complicated forms like the fugue were abandoned, and, in light of the shifting fashions, Bach's work would be forgotten for many years once he was no longer around to keep it alive.

Bach began writing *The Art of Fugue* in 1742 but was not able to complete it before he died. As a result, the work leaves a number of questions unanswered, including whether it was even meant to be played. Bach may very well have intended the work as an exploration into the theory of composition, the musical equivalent of a research project. It is certainly possible to play the music, but uncertain whether or not that was its primary purpose.

*The Art of Fugue* also serves, in a way, as Bach's epitaph. The final section contains an autograph—the composer has written his own name into the piece. This was a fairly common practice and accomplished by using the note B-flat (to stand for the letter B), A and C, and then B-natural (a German H). What makes this episode unique is that the music stops abruptly after the letter H. Carl Philipp Emanuel later wrote on the manuscript page, "While working on this fugue, where the name BACH is introduced...the author died."

Bach's eyesight had begun failing him in 1747, when he was sixty-three years old. Much of the problem stemmed from too many late nights studying manuscripts by candlelight, a habit he began as a boy. However, at this point in his life the strain on his eyes became so severe he could barely see at all. He was also in a great deal of pain. His wife and a secretary helped him write letters and copy music. Many documents from these last years of his life merely feature his scratchy signature. The few things he did write are very shaky and messy, as though he had to be very close to the paper in order to see what he was doing.

One does not die of poor eyesight, so it is speculated that Bach actually suffered from diabetes, which can negatively affect vision. Diabetes had not yet been discovered, so it would have gone untreated. Once it became clear that Bach's health was not going to get better, the town council of Leipzig decided to hold auditions for a new cantor. They wanted someone they liked and who would be cooperative to take over Bach's duties. It was in the poorest taste to hold these auditions or to appoint someone while the current cantor still lived, and Bach demonstrated his ire by continuing to work. He found enough energy to direct several concerts in the summer of 1749 and performed at his daughter Elisabeth's wedding in January of 1750. She was the only one of his four daughters to marry.

When the pain in his eyes became unbearable, Bach decided to take a serious risk. In February of 1750, he hired a man named Chevalier John Taylor, the eye doctor to King George II in England, to remove the cataracts on his eyes. This was a highly experimental procedure, as, back then, surgery was nothing like the safe, sterile process it is today. It seemed a miracle that after the operation Bach's eyesight did, in fact, improve, but the good results were short-lived. Two weeks later, the pain was worse than ever and the blindness almost complete. Bach opted to try the surgery a second time.

This was a fatal mistake. Infection made his eyes swell and poisoned his circulatory system. He was nearly paralyzed and completely blind for the last six months of his life. Meanwhile, Dr. Taylor made a hasty retreat to England where, sadly, he would wind up doing the same damage to composer George Frideric Handel nine years later.

On July 18, 1750, Bach awakened to find that he could see his family gathered around him. All of his loved ones prayed that this might mean he was on the mend. Over the next ten days, however, he suffered a series of strokes, the last of which was about two hours before his death on July 28 at about 8:00 P.M.

The funeral took place three days later without cost to the Bach family. The entire student body and faculty

*S. Johannis Kirche mit dem neu gebauten Thurn.*

Johann Sebastian Bach was buried here, at St. John's Church in Leipzig. *(Courtesy of Bach Archiv, Leipzig.)*

of St. Thomas School, his family, and friends all attended. Bach's longtime friend and musical colleague, Georg Philipp Telemann wrote a touching eulogy: "Then sleep! The candle of thy fame ne'er low will burn; the pupils thou hast trained, and those they train in turn prepare thy future crown of glory brightly glowing."

Bach was buried in the cemetery on the south side of St. John's Church, but no marker was placed to designate his resting place. It is assumed his remains lie about six paces from the southern church door, for on July 28 of every year for the next century, the students of St. Thomas would gather there to remember Johann Sebastian Bach, the cantor who had changed the school and town—and music itself—forever.

# Chapter Nine
## The Revival

Anna Magdalena Bach had only six months to remove her belongings and children from the living quarters at St. Thomas School. Bach had never saved much money, choosing to spend what he earned on building his music library and collecting clavier instruments. What little he had was divvied out between his widow and the nine surviving children. The Leipzig town council gave Anna Magdalena a small pension, but that soon ran out. After a couple years of begging for more money and selling some of her husband's original manuscripts to the school at a very meager price, Anna Magdalena finally had to give up custody of her children. She could no longer afford to take care of them. J. Gottlieb Görner took the youngest four into his care, and Johann Christian Bach went to live with his brother Carl Philipp

Emanuel in Berlin until he was old enough to be out on his own. In 1760, Anna Magdalena, living on welfare, died and was buried in the same cemetery as her husband. She probably does not lie next to him, because by this time no one was sure exactly where Bach's body had been put to rest ten years earlier.

Only thirty copies of *The Art of Fugue* were sold when it was finally published in 1756. It seemed nobody was much interested in Bach's techniques, and the style of music Bach preferred to write was out of fashion. To say the name Bach in the latter half of the eighteenth century would be to refer to one of Sebastian's four sons, who had prominent musical careers of their own. The oldest, Wilhelm Friedemann, squandered his career through lack of self-discipline and died an impoverished alcoholic in 1795. Younger brothers Johann Christoph Friedrich and Johann Christian had good, steady careers, the first one as a composer of chamber music, the other as a composer of concertos in England. The most famous of the sons was Carl Philipp Emanuel, whose symphonic works paved the way for the classical masters Joseph Haydn, Wolfgang Amadeus Mozart, and Ludwig van Beethoven. Though Carl Philipp Emanuel worked very hard to keep the memory of his father alive, even writing a long obituary and granting interviews to J. Nicolaus Forkel, Bach's first biographer, only a handful of people still recognized the name of J. Sebastian Bach.

Even in Leipzig, Bach was soon a dim memory. In a time before musicians were revered as artists, each new composer would simply throw out the works of the old one when the new person took over a position. Bach had every reason to believe most of his works would die when he did. It is a quirk of history that one of Bach's former students took over his role as cantor at St. Thomas School in 1755. The student made frequent use of his former master's chorale music. In 1789, Wolfgang Amadeus Mozart, came to Leipzig and happened to hear one of Bach's pieces sung by the St. Thomas choir. Mozart was stunned at what he heard. An eyewitness said this:

> Hardly had the choir sung a few measures when Mozart sat up, startled; a few measures more and he called out "what is this?" And now his whole soul seemed to be in his ears. When the singing was finished he cried out, full of joy: "Now there is something one can learn from!" He was told that this school, in which Sebastian Bach had been Cantor, possessed the complete collection of his motets and preserved them as a sort of sacred relic. "That's the spirit! That's fine!" he cried. "Let's see them!" There was, however, no score of these songs; so he had the parts given to him; and then it was for the silent observer a joy to see how eagerly Mozart sat himself down, with the parts all around him—in both hands, on his knees, and on the chairs next to him—and forgetting everything else, did not get up until he had looked through everything of Bach's that was there.

Mozart's initial reaction to Bach became the basis for

Wolfgang Amadeus Mozart was among the composers who would be deeply impressed and influenced by Bach's intricate compositions. *(Courtesy of Internationale Stiftung Mozarteum, Salzburg.)*

a life-long admiration. It was Bach's synthesis of different genres which set the stage for Mozart's own signature blending. It is likely Mozart had a copy of the *Well-tempered Clavier* next to his own piano, and for years Mozart would join a group of friends to listen to nothing but Bach and Haydn every Sunday.

Such reverence was not exclusive to Mozart. Ludwig van Beethoven made his first public performance in Vienna at age eleven playing most of the *Well-tempered Clavier*. Later, he used the book to instruct his own students and collected as many of Bach's extant works as he could find. When Beethoven heard that Bach's last surviving daughter, Regina Susanna, was growing old in poverty, he donated to her the proceeds from one of his publications.

Although the respect of these great masters was genuine, it hardly accounts for why Bach's works are so revered today. His complicated counterpoint and clavier studies were still only known and appreciated by other musicians—not by the music-loving public. It would take the fascination and hard work of yet another musical genius to make J. S. Bach a household name.

Felix Mendelssohn-Bartholdy was barely a teenager when two of his friends, Robert Schumann, a teacher at Leipzig University, and Carl Zelter, a choir director, introduced him to the music of J. S. Bach. Mendelssohn had been a child prodigy and by the age of fourteen had already composed symphonies, concertos, piano music, and two operas. As a Christmas present in 1823,

Mendelssohn's grandmother bought him a copy of Bach's *St. Matthew Passion,* and Mendelssohn spent the next five years wheeling and dealing in order to have it performed. He was twenty years old when he finally conducted the masterpiece in Berlin, exactly one hundred years after its premiere. The performance astonished the public. "There was a crowd and a noise," wrote Mendelssohn, "the like of which I have never experienced at a concert of sacred music."

Robert Schumann, the great composer, and Mendelssohn together founded the Bach Society and put on a series of concerts to raise money for the building of a monument to Bach in Leipzig. The Bach Society made it a prime goal to categorize and publish all of the late composer's works. Few of the pieces had ever been published, so it was a laborious forty-nine-year task to locate all of the original manuscripts and have them transcribed. The process was finally completed in the year 1900, long after both Mendelssohn and Schumann had died. The massive collection was numbered and labeled with the letters BWV, for the German title "Bach Werke Verzeichnis" (Bach Work Collection). Truly the *oeuvre* of a master, Bach's collected works glorifies almost every genre of the Baroque age of music, with opera being the major exception.

Today Bach is considered the greatest of the great, the first of the three B's of classical music, a group that also includes Beethoven and Brahms. His *Well-tempered Clavier* and *The Art of Fugue* are required reading for every

Johann Sebastian Bach (1685-1750). *(Courtesy of Museum für Geschichte der Stadt Leipzig.)*

serious student of music. Works by Bach are recorded and played everywhere, even appearing in jazz and new age music. Arrangements of Bach's work have been made for every conceivable instrument (a necessary thing considering that harpsichords have become obsolete and pipe organs are few and far between). In 1977, selected recordings of Bach's music were transported on the unmanned spaceship Voyager and launched into outer space as an example of our civilization to possible alien cultures. Johann Sebastian Bach may not have been entirely appreciated in his lifetime, but he has left behind a rich legacy that will continue to inspire for centuries.

# Timeline

1685    Johann Sebastian Bach is born in Eisenach, Germany, on March 21.

1694    Bach's mother dies.

1695    Bach's father remarries, dies shortly thereafter; Bach moves to Ohrdruf to live with older brother.

1700    Attends St. Michael's monastery school in Lüneburg.

1702    Leaves school to audition for work.

1703    In January, is hired by Duke Johann Ernst in Weimar; in July, is hired as organist at New Church in Arnstadt.

1707    Becomes organist at St. Blasius Church in Mühlhausen; marries Maria Barbara on October 17.

1708    In June, is offered a position as capellmeister to Duke Wilhelm Ernst of Weimar; Catharina Dorothea, the first of Bach's 20 children, born.

1710    Son Wilhelm Friedemann born.

1714    Son Carl Philipp Emanuel born.

1715    Son Johann Gottfried Bernhard born.

1717    Bach plays harpsichord duel with Marchan le Grand in Dresden; in November, Bach is put in Weimar jail for disobedience; in December, Bach and his family move to Cothen to work in court of Prince Leopold.

1718    Son Leopold Augustus born.

1719   Son Leopold Augustus dies.

1720   Bach travels to Carlsbad with Prince Leopold; Maria
Barbara, Bach's first wife, dies while he's away.

1721   Bach marries Anna Magdelena Wülcken; completes
the *Brandenburg Concertos.*

1722   Composes *The Well-Tempered Clavier.*

1723   Composes *St. John Passion* for Leipzig audition; in
May, Bach takes position as Cantor at St. Thomas
School in Leipzig; daughter Christiana Sophia Henrietta
born.

1724   Son Gottfried Heinrich born.

1725   Son Christian Gottlieb born.

1726   Daughter Elizabeth Juliana Friederica born; C. Sophia
Henrietta dies.

1727   Son Ernestus Andreas born and dies.

1728   Son Christian Gottlieb dies; Regina Johanna born.

1729   Premieres *St. Matthew Passion* in Leipzig; becomes
director of the collegium musicum.

1730   Daughter Christiana Benedicta born and dies.

1731   Daughter Christiana Dorothea born.

1732   Son Johann Christoph Griedrich born, C. Dorothea
dies.

1733   Composes *Mass in B-minor,* but it is not performed.

1734   Composes *Christmas Oratorio.*

1735   Son Johann Christian born.

1737   Daughter Johanna Carolina born.

1742   Finishes composing *Clavier-Übung* "Goldberg Variations;" daughter Regina Susanna born.

1747   Plays before King Frederick II, of Prussia; composes *A
Musical Offering* for the King; completes *The Art of
Fugue.*

1750   Johann Sebastian Bach dies of complications from eye
surgery on July 28.

# Glossary of Musical Terms

**apprentice** One who works for a master in exchange for education.

**audition** The process of trying out for work as a musician.

**Baroque era** A period in history that dates roughly from 1600 to 1750. The most famous composers from this era are Bach, Vivaldi, and Handel.

**bass** The deepest voice in a choir.

**bassoon** A deep-toned woodwind instrument.

**cantata** A religious play without scenery or staging that is sung by a choir, usually with soloists and an orchestra.

**cantor** The teacher of a school and/or church choir and orchestra.

**capelle** The orchestra employed by a noble court.

**capellmeister** The director of music for a town or noble court. Also the conductor of a musical ensemble (capelle).

**choir** An ensemble of singers singing in harmony (also called a *chorus*).

**choristers** The members of a choir.

**chorale** A song that is sung by a choir—usually part of a cantata or oratorio.

**clavier** An instrument with a keyboard (i.e.: harpsichord, piano, organ).

**composer** One who writes music.

**concerto** A piece of instrumental music which highlights a particular instrument.

**counterpoint** The craft of composing simultaneous melodies.

**currende** Begging for money by singing in the streets.

**equal temperament** To have all the strings of a keyboard in tune with each other (also known as well-tempered).

**fugue** A musical form in which an initial melody is changed, rearranged, and repeated many times in many different voices to produce a complicated, tapestry-like texture.

**harpsichord** A keyboard instrument in which the strings are plucked by quills.

**hymns** The religious songs sung in a church service.

**magnificat** A musical setting of a hymn in the Bible sung by the Virgin Mary.

**manuscript** Music written out on paper, either published or bound (also known as a score).

**Mass** The central service of the Roman Catholic Church.

**modulate** When the music moves from one key to another.

**motets** Compositions for multiple voices without musical accompaniment.

**oboe** A double-reed woodwind instrument.

**oeuvre** A substantial body of work, made up of the lifework of a writer, artist, or composer.

**opera** Originating in seventeenth-century Italy, a story set to music, usually entirely sung. Music, drama, scenery, costumes, dance, and other theatrical elements combine to make the art form complete.

**orchestra** A group of instruments divided into wind, brass, percussion, and string sections.

**organ** A large keyboard instrument, whose sound is made by pushing wind through tall pipes.

**organist** One who plays the organ.

**partita** An instrumental piece for dancing.

**passion** A large-scale cantata about the life and death of Jesus Christ (usually performed at Easter).

**pianoforte** The full name for the piano, literally meaning "soft loud." Because their chords are struck with hammers (rather than plucked, as is the case with the piano's predecessor, the harpsichord), pianos are capable of producing a great range of volume and expressiveness.

**repertoire** The list of pieces a certain group or soloist knows how to play.

**royalties** The fees collected by the artist for the sale and performance of his work.

**sacred** From or having to do with the church.

**secular** Not connected to religion.

**serenata** A dramatic cantata. The name is like that of a *serenade* (which is an outdoor piece) because it also took place outside, though usually at night.

**solo** A piece of music that is played or sung by a single performer.

**sonata** A composition for a solo or accompanied instrument, usually in three or four movements of varying tempo.

**soprano** The highest voice in a choir.

**syncopation** The deliberate shifting of the accent from the main beat to a weak beat or an off-beat, resulting in an unexpected change in the meter or pulse of a piece of music.

**virtuoso** An expert performer on a particular instrument.

# *Sources*

**CHAPTER TWO: "The Organs of Lüneburg"**

p. 39, "could not praise the beauty…"Christoph Wolff, *Johann Sebastian Bach: The Learned Musician* (New York: W.W. Norton & Company, 2000), 63.

**CHAPTER THREE: "Getting Work"**

p. 44, "lackey," Wolff, *Johann Sebastian Bach,* 68.

p. 49, "dirty dog," Hans T. David and Arthur Mendel (ed.), *The Bach Reader: A Life of Johann Sebastian Bach in Letters and Documents* (New York: W.W. Norton & Company, Inc., 1966), 51.

p. 34, "he must get along with the students…" Ibid., 51.

p. 49, "appear promptly on Sundays…" Ibid., 50.

p. 50, "…hoped the organ playing had been so well taken care of…" Ibid., 51.

p. 51, "…having hitherto made many curious *variationes*…" Ibid., 51.

p. 52, "he must not be ashamed to make music with the students" Ibid., 52.

**CHAPTER FOUR: "Church Music"**

p. 58, "little council piece," Wolff, *Johann Sebastian Bach,* 110.

p. 61, "Your Magnificence, Honored and Noble Sirs..." David, *Bach Reader,* 60.

## CHAPTER FIVE: "Dealing with Dukes"

p. 73, "It is not to be assumed..." Wolff, *Johann Sebastian Bach,* 154.

p. 74, "His organ and clavier compositions..." Klaus Eidam, Hoyt Rogers, (trans.) *The True Life of JS Bach* (New York: Basic Books, 2001), 86.

p. 78, "County Judge's place of detention" David, *Bach Reader,* 75.

p. 78, "freed from arrest with notice of his unfavorable discharge." Ibid 75.

## CHAPTER SIX "A Time of Friendship and Love"

p. 84, "I thought this art was dead..." Carmel Berman Reingold, *Immortals of Music: Johann Sebastian Bach, Revolutionary of Music* (New York: Franklin Watts, Inc., 1970), 59.

p. 85, "If such conditions are to prevail in our city..." Hendrik Willem Van Loon, *The Life and Times of Johann Sebastian Bach* (New York: Simon and Schuster, 1940), 37.

## CHAPTER SEVEN: "Classes and Cantatas"

p. 92, "Last Saturday at noon..." David, *Bach Reader,* 92.

p. 96, "with good applause," Wolff, *Johann Sebastian Bach,* 245.

p. 98, "seventeen are competent, twenty not yet fully..." Michael Sartorius, *Baroque Composers and Musicians: Johann Sebastian Bach, a detailed informative biography* (Arton Baroque Music Pages, 1998), 12.

p. 102, "Jesus, help me." Katherine B. Shippen and Anca Seidlova, *The Heritage of Music* (New York: The Viking Press, 1963), 87.

p. 103, "He did not care, for he got nothing out of it anyway…" Bettmann, *Johann Sebastian Bach,* 172.

p. 103, "The choirmaster does nothing!" Eidam, *The True Life of JS Bach,* 221.

p. 104, "…at first, indeed, it did not seem at all proper to me…" David, *Bach Reader,* 125.

**CHAPTER EIGHT: "The Final Years"**

p. 107, "They are born musicians…" Reingold, *Immortals of Music,* 82.

p. 109, "notwithstanding the main tendency of his genius…" Wolff, *Johann Sebastian Bach,* 361.

p. 115, "The situation between him and Ernesti…" Ibid., 350.

p. 116, "What shall I say or do further?" Ibid., 400.

p. 117, "Dear Goldberg, do play me my variations." Bettmann, *Johann Sebastian Bach,* 88.

p. 120, "While working on this fugue…" Malcolm Boyd, *Bach.* (New York: Oxford University Press, 2000), 223.

p. 122, "Then sleep! The candle of thy fame…" Ibid., 193.

**CHAPTER NINE: "The Revival"**

p. 125, "Hardly had the choir sung a few measures when Mozart sat up…" David, *Bach Reader,* 359-60.

p. 128, "There was a crowd and a noise…" Ibid., 371.

# Bibliography

Bettmann, Otto L. *Johann Sebastian Bach, As His World Knew Him*. New York: Birch Lane Press, Carol Publishing Group, 1995.

Boyd, Malcom. *The Master Musicians: Bach*. Oxford: Oxford University Press, 2000.

Burkofzer, Manfred F. *Music in the Baroque Era*. New York: W.W. Norton & Company, Inc., 1947.

Carlin, Richard. *European Classical Music 1600-1825*. New York and Oxford: Facts on File Publishing, 1988.

Catucci, Stefano. *Masters of Music: Bach and Baroque Music*. New York: Barron's Educational Series, Inc., 1997.

Cavalletti, Carlo. *Masters of Music: Chopin and Romantic Music*. New York: Barron's Educational Series, Inc., 2000.

Chiapusso, Jan. *Bach's World*. Bloomington and London: Indiana University Press, 1968.

David, Hans T. and Arthur Mendel (ed.). *The Bach Reader: A Life of Johann Sebastian Bach in Letters and Documents*. New York: W.W. Norton & Company, Inc., 1966.

Eidam, Klaus. (Hoyt Rogers, trans.) *The True Life of JS Bach*. New York: Basic Books, 2001.

Fulbrook, Mary. *A Concise History of Germany*. Cambridge: Cambridge University Press, 1990.

Geiringer, Karl. *Johann Sebastian Bach: The Culmination of an Era*. New York: Oxford University Press, 1966.

Reingold, Carmel Berman. *Immortals of Music: Johann Sebastian Bach, Revolutionary of Music*. New York: Franklin Watts, Inc., 1970.

Russell, Francis. *The Horizon Concise History of Germany*. New York: American Heritage Publishing Co., Inc., 1973.

Sadie, Stanley. *The New Grove Dictionary of Music and Musicians*. Washington, D.C.: Macmillan Publishers Limited, 1980.

Sartorius, Michael. *Baroque Composers and Musicians: Johann Sebastian Bach, a detailed informative biography*. (Arton Baroque Music Pages. 1998.)

Schweitzer, Albert. *JS Bach*. New York: Dover Publications, 1966.

Seidlova, Anca and Katherine B. Shippen. *The Heritage of Music*. New York: The Viking Press, 1963.

Spitta, Philipp. *Johann Sebastian Bach*. New York: Dover Publications, 1951.

Van Loon, Hendrik Willem. *The Life and Times of Johann Sebastian Bach*. New York: Simon and Schuster, 1940.

Wolff, Christoph. *Johann Sebastian Bach: The Learned Musician*. New York: W.W. Norton & Company, 2000.

# Web sites

**Baroque Composers and Musicians**
http://www.baroquemusic.org

**The Canons and Fugues of J.S. Bach, by Timothy A. Smith**
http://jan.ucc.nau.edu/~tas3/bachindex.html

**Humanities Web**
http://www.humanitiesweb.org

**The Internet Public Library's Music History 102 (A guide to Western composers and their music from the Middle Ages to the present)**
http://www.ipl.org/div/mushist

# *Index*